TIME MALL

MARK JORDAN

LIBERTY HILL PUBLISHING

Liberty Hill Publishing
555 Winderley Pl, Suite 225
Maitland, FL 32751
407.339.4217
www.libertyhillpublishing.com

© 2024 by Mark Jordan

All rights reserved solely by the author. The author guarantees all contents are original and do not infringe upon the legal rights of any other person or work. No part of this book may be reproduced in any form without the permission of the author.

Due to the changing nature of the Internet, if there are any web addresses, links, or URLs included in this manuscript, these may have been altered and may no longer be accessible. The views and opinions shared in this book belong solely to the author and do not necessarily reflect those of the publisher. The publisher therefore disclaims responsibility for the views or opinions expressed within the work.

Paperback ISBN-13: 978-1-66289-949-2
Ebook ISBN-13: 978-1-66289-950-8

PROLOGUE
"Checking In On Time"

The Dawn of Man

A group of frozen and grimy Neanderthals huddle around the dying remnants of a feeble attempt at fire. Despair and gloom hang in the air, along with the putrid smoke. These men are more dead than alive.

Suddenly there is a flash of orange light and an energized cave dweller bursts onto the scene. He is bearing a most curious item that he places atop a large rock. It is a shiny metal boombox. All gather around it with a mixture of fear and curiosity.

The group pokes and prods the mysterious object. At last, the proper button is pushed, and a bump and grind tune starts to play. There are shouts and shrieks of terror, along with some bowel evacuations, most back off, but as the music continues, the motley crew is pulled back in.

A fur-covered lovely emerges from the crowd. She jumps onto the rock beside the boombox and begins to dance. The eyes of the men are riveted to her. She removes one layer of fur after another until she is left with, for all practical purposes, a fur bikini. The two fur strips strain to conceal her femininity as the guys go wild.

Now the top comes off. Her huge, dirty, delightful breasts are revealed. She is indeed the mother of all mankind.

The males are now in a crazed state. They start picking up small stones and shoving them into her bikini bottom. She quickly accumulates so many that she loses her balance and falls into the crowd. Thus ends the world's first striptease.

Florence, Italy - 1505

Leonardo Da Vinci is busy in his workshop. He is painting on the Mona Lisa, working from sketches that are scattered about. After a bout of furious activity, he puts down his brush and picks up a large sandwich. It is a Subway Meatball Marinara.

The master takes a bite and looks pleased. He studies the aesthetics of the foot long then takes another bite. He finds it delicious and utters an appropriate exclamation:

"Magnifico!"

Leonardo puts down the sandwich and studies his work. Then he reaches into the pocket of his smock, retrieving an object that requires intense deliberation. It is a spent Federal 12-gauge shotgun shell that once contained a load of #4 buckshot.

After ten to twelve minutes, he puts the shell back in his pocket and resumes painting. The Mona Lisa is coming along nicely.

The Alamo
March 6, 1836
Early Morning

The battle for the Alamo is almost over but Davy Crockett still fights. Long after he ran out of black powder and had to wield his .40 caliber flintlock as a deadly club. Long after the gun disintegrated while bashing the heads of a smarmy sergeant and his creepy corporal. Long after his knife fell apart while fileting about a dozen attackers like Tennessee river carp. Now things are hand-to-hand, and Crockett is a fighting machine. He administers a right to a Juan, a left to a Pablo, and a kick in the crotch to an Alejandro.

Crocket fights his way to the front door of the chapel. He opens the door and stares back at the approaching horde, longing for the weapon he left behind:

"I sure wish I had brung up Old Betsy with me."

Crockett slams the door hard, and the Mexicans swarm it, but the force of Crockett's slam has jammed it shut and they can't get it open. A moment later a flash of orange light illuminates the area as Davy bursts through the roof and hovers in mid-air as he is now strapped to a Bell Rocket Belt from the 1960s. His head is protected by a vintage Houston Oilers football helmet with the tail of his coonskin cap protruding from underneath. There is a flintlock rifle slung across the control arms. His attackers stare in stunned amazement as Crockett delivers a parting remark:

"Kiss my ass you bastards! See you at San Jacinto."

With that, Davy Crockett, aware of his twenty-one seconds of fuel, shoots out of sight as the soldiers fall to their knees in prayer.

December 9, 1945
Near Mannheim, Germany

General Patton's 1938 Cadillac Model 75 is slicing through the cold German morning. He is more than two hours out from his headquarters in Bad Nauheim and headed toward a pheasant hunt in the woods near Speyer. George is clad in his personal uniform of a short-waisted olive drab jacket, khaki shirt and tie with matching jodhpurs and highly polished black riding boots. A pair of ivory-handled revolvers flank his hips. On his right is a Colt .45 Model 1873 SAA (Single Action Army). On his left is a Smith and Wesson "registered magnum," later to be called a Model 27. His helmet is stowed away, along with the hunting equipment, in the support jeep that travels just behind.

George Patton has had a good day so far. He has spent some time in the front passenger seat talking to his driver, an earnest, young PFC from Kentucky who has recently reenlisted to continue his role as Patton's chauffer. There has been a stop near Salzburg to view Roman ruins and an encounter with a proactive MP at a checkpoint close to Viernheim that brought a smile to the General's face.

Now he is in the rear seat alternately talking to his chief-of-staff, General Hobart "Hap" Gay, who sits on his left, and looking out the window pondering theoretical troop placements to fit the passing scenery.

The little convoy has now entered the suburb of Neckarstadt via Bundesautobahn (Federal Highway) 38. They come upon a railroad crossing as a train approaches. Patton's driver carefully stops to wait it out.

The train passes, and the PFC guns the Caddy across the tracks. Then the jeep passes the General's car to take the point the rest of the way to the hunting grounds. The alert PFC takes note of a large army supply truck approaching from the opposite direction. An army quartermaster depot is passed on the right, and Patton points out the wartime debris piled around it.

Suddenly, without the driver even signaling, the truck, a two-and-a-half-ton GMC 6x6, turns in front of the oncoming car. Patton's driver hits the brakes but it is too late. There is a flash of orange light and then the Cadillac plows into the passenger side of the truck smashing the auto's grille and right front fender.

History has long recorded severe neck injuries and a lingering death twelve days later for George Patton as a result of this accident.

However, as General Gay and the driver shake off the effects of the wreck, they realize General Patton is not in the car. They enlist the services of the sergeant who was driving the jeep and the three men from the truck to search for him, per chance he has been thrown clear, but he is nowhere to be found.

Four-star General George Smith Patton, Jr. has disappeared.

pops ajar one inch; he opens it with his left hand and steps in, shutting it behind him in one smooth move. He looks down the hallway ahead of him still amazed that he has gotten away with that password for so long.

As he starts to traverse the hall the first open door on the left is that of the sports department. He waves to those guys as he walks by. They are some of the good people at the station who don't get involved in the daily power struggle.

The next door on the left is that of his boss and enemy, Burley Dick, the production manager. He carefully peeks around the door frame and is pleased to find that the office is empty. This puts a smile on his face and he decides to look for his friend, Steve Love, who is probably in the breakroom.

Mark does a one-eighty and enters the short hallway between master control on the left and the newsroom on the right, a snippet of audio drifts out of master and catches his ear. It is the end of a commercial he has written, *"The Crowe Furniture Company. Fly on over or give us a caaawwww! So, you can lay the best furniture in your nest for the lowest prices! And visit our latest store at the exciting, new Taj Ma-Mall in the former Biggsley neighborhood."* He shakes his head in disgust at what he has written and because of his issues with the Taj Ma-Mall.

He makes a left turn and enters the hallway that

runs between the news edit suites on his left and production control on his right. He glances up at the dusty, yellow stained ceiling. Smoking is now banned in the building (except for the general manager's office) but the nicotine archive remains.

He carefully passes production control. Even though the door is closed, he can still hear Burley Dick's voice inside haranguing the day crew over some triviality. Mark rushes past and enters the lower lobby. This is where guests on the station's low-rated morning show, *Wolf Down Your Breakfast*, await their turn while sitting on uncomfortable furniture provided by the Crowe Furniture Company.

The lobby is quiet at the moment as someone has turned off the television that is supposed to remain on and tuned to WDOA at all times per the orders of the chain-smoking general manager Will Veal. (This order is seldom carried out by the rank-and-file.) As Mark looks around the room, his eyes are drawn, as usual, to an ancient poster hanging crooked in the back corner that proclaims the 'programming revolution' of the Wolf Television Network. A revolution that was put down long ago. The poster has a cracked plastic cover and is caked with dust. It has long been forgotten by the comatose promotions department.

Mark adjusts the position of the black Bic Stic Pen (medium tip) in his shirt pocket then looks at the poster; he is pleased, as usual, that his reflection is staring back at him through the dust. He likes what he sees. The dark brown hair ("Just for Men" is a fine product) halfway covering his perfectly sized ears with small, attached lobes. The green eyes. The Stafford red and white striped oxford (purchased from a now woke store that Mark no longer shops at) with its long sleeves rolled halfway up and the tail out (his one concession to the sloppiness of the era) hanging over his black (reversable to brown) leather belt from George and black Rustler jeans out of Wrangler. Black nylon socks also via George and solid black New Balance shoes complete the ensemble. Mark likes to buy items from George because it lets him think about George Washington while standing in the men's department of Walmart amid the Chinese products he knows Mr. Washington would have no use for. Pushing fifty and looking good, Mark thinks to himself. Now to see if Steve is in the breakroom.

Steve Love had entered the breakroom minutes earlier after checking out his own image in the poster. He is a talented videographer now relegated to running studio camera for various newscasts as punishment for his disdain of authority and carefree attitude. Recently turned fifty, he still has most of his blondish hair and only a couple of specks of gray in his beard. (Yes, Mark has told him that "Just for Men" has a beard and moustache version, but he is ok with the gray for now.) His midsection is sometimes troublesome, but a vigorous walking program is keeping it in check. And he is as virile as a clowder of tomcats in a catnip patch, having been married four times and divorced four times. He has one son from each wife and has received very few Father's Day cards for his trouble.

Steve likes to wear message T-shirts and today's choice features the iconic yellow and black Gadsden flag, "DON'T TREAD ON ME." Underneath the shirt hangs a gold chain linked to a small Christian cross around his neck. The look is well accessorized by his Lee stonewashed jeans, his "chick magnet" cotton socks (pictures of baby chickens and magnets) from Sock Harbor, and his white Nikes.

As he enters the breakroom, he is pleased that Arnie, the evening newscast director, has a fresh pot of coffee brewed and awaiting him on the Bunn coffee maker. He glances at the rack of employee coffee mugs on the wall and gives them the finger of his right hand. Nan Carpy, the assistant news director has banned Styrofoam cups from the building and decreed that all employees must drink from their own individual mug. And since Carpy's picture happens to be hanging on the wall as the current "EMPLOYEE OF THE MONTH" he gives her the finger with his left hand as he reaches his right into the narrow crevice between the right of the protruding wall and the left of the refrigerator. (Steve can flip the bird well with either hand while Mark only uses his right.) He pulls out a mop, something the contract cleaning crew would never use, and sets it aside, he then pulls out a sleeve of extra-large Styrofoam cups, his personal stash, he takes one cup from the sleeve and restores the previous setup.

As a steaming cup is poured, Steve is a bit apprehensive as rumors have been floating around the station of a new coffee provider. He takes one large sip, swishes it around his mouth, and is pleased as he recognizes it as Colombian from the Risaralda department in the Paisa region. Some people prefer the fruitier blends grown at the higher altitudes to the south in the Nariño region, but this java fan knows that for robust flavor the coffee triangle cannot be beaten.

He walks to the farthest away of the three round tables, sets down his cup and picks up a copy of the day's newspaper that is laying there. Still standing he reads through it for a bit, it is mostly coverage of the recently opened Taj Ma-mall. He tosses the paper down, walks over to the vending machine, and spots more good fortune because there is a rare to WDOA—two pack of Twinkies located between Will Veal's Lucky Strikes and Nan Carpy's crappy, cranberry, calorie-free, crusty crepes. Some management types are allowed to have favorite items stocked in the machine. Mark and Steve have no such privilege.

Steve sends three quarters rattling down the coin chute one after another, a 2002 Tennessee, a 2007 South Carolina, and a 1993 only representing the fact of being a quarter. He carefully enters the code B-9, avoiding the Lucky Strikes at B-8 and the Carpy crappy bars at B-10. The coil holding his prize turns and the Twinkies land in the receiving tray with a delicious thud. He retrieves the golden duo and returns to the table where his coffee awaits, the metal and plastic chair making a squeak on the cracked linoleum as it is pulled into position.

Mr. Love is now seated with the Twinkies face down in front of him. Time to go to work. He surgically opens the pack, lifts the cardboard, wipes the gunk off it with his right middle finger and licks it off. He sets the cardboard down and savors the preview. The taste seems excellent. Could it be? Steve has long suspected that Lewisburg was being shipped Twinkies from the Emporia Kansas plant, which is fine, however … Steve takes a bite from the first golden sponge cake and … yes, the cellulose gum, the high fructose corn syrup, the soy lecithin, this Twinkie was baked at the Shadeland avenue facility in Indianapolis. In fact, it's from Mr. Norman's second-shift crew as they have a special way of spicing up the polysorbate 60.

He finishes the first Twinkie and picks up the second as Mark enters the room with a friendly, "Hi!" Steve precisely breaks the treat in two and tosses half to Mark, "Have a Twinkie, bro!" who catches it and pops it into his mouth in one slick move.

"That's good," Mark states. "Shadeland avenue?"

"You got it roadie." Steve is happy that he has trained Mark well in Twinkieology but now remembers something somber, "Sorry to hear about your cat."

"Thank you. Eighteen years is pretty good for a cat, but you always want more.

"Her name was Moo?"

Mark ponders wistfully, "Yeah, she was white with black patches like a Holstein."

"I heard Larry used to send her emails." He rescues a couple of twinkie crumbs from the table with his right middle finger and deposits them in his mouth.

"And he would leave her messages on my answering machine."

"Dude!" Steve is incredulous at the reminder that Mark still has an answering machine. "We've got to get you a cell phone."

"It's down to me and a guy in the jungle in the Philippines who don't have them," Mark answers pridefully, "and I intend to wait him out."

Steve shakes his head and picks up the newspaper. "I still can't believe they tore down Larry's whole neighborhood to build a shopping mall. That thing went up fast."

Mark now shakes his head, "After we helped Larry move, I stayed away from there. I did not want to see any of the destruction or construction. And I do mean con." He lets out a sigh. "Larry's ancestors settled that area."

"They defeated that Indian chief," Steve thinks it out, "... oh ... uh ... Don-ee-o. Chief Don-ee-o."

"He was the most powerful Shawnee chief in the area," Mark knows the history.

Steve points to a couple of pictures in the paper, "Here are the bastards who destroyed Biggsley, Garmon Spooneybarger, and Nelson Trafalgar; I guess he's English or something."

Mark starts to bristle. "He's something, but he's not English."

"The English guy is not English, what is he?"

"Fictitious. And Spooneybarger is a nut job. We used to call him 'Looneyburger.'"

"Whoa, you know them or him or what the hell?

Mark starts to ponder a painful story that has many bizarre twists and turns. He frequently likes to hide from reality by watching Me TV and collecting pictures of actresses, living and dead, in bikinis, but this story is back in a big way so it must be told. "Notice there are two separate pictures. There is only one guy, Garmon Spooneybarger. He doesn't like to admit that he's from Hanktown, but he was in my high school class. He lived in my neighborhood. His father ran a crooked construction company, the company Spooney runs today, so they had a little money. After his freshman year, his dad took the family to London, England, for the summer. It made an impression on Spooney. Word was that he got a blowjob from a Manchester tart within sight of the Lord Nelson statue in Trafalgar square."

"I love Manchester tarts almost as much as Twinkies," Steve chimes in.

Mark continues, "When he returned for our sophomore year, he declared himself to be 'Nelson Trafalgar' and wore a fancy English outfit, waistcoat, striped pants, vest, bowler hat, fake accent, and he always carried an umbrella. He looked like the ambassador to the Twilight Zone."

"Wow," Steve ponders the story. "Did anyone try to beat the fuck out of him or anything?"

"The football team tried for a while, but Spooney became so adept at wielding the umbrella as a weapon that he was a threat to gouge out eyeballs. By the middle of the season the offensive line had only four good eyes between them, and Nelson Trafalgar was being left alone. By the end of sophomore year Garmon Spooneybarger was back, and Nelson Trafalgar was mostly gone, except for special occasions, like the senior prom. But that's another story."

"Hmm," Steve ponders the story then changes gears, "let's go talk to Larry."

"Let's do it." Mark welcomes the opportunity.

Steve jumps to his feet and stuffs his Twinkie

debris into the trash can. Then they exit the breakroom and head to the elevator a few feet away. But before Steve can push the down button they are approached from their left by Biff LaFolluvette and Nan Carpy who have just entered the lower lobby.

Biff LaFolluvette is the news director. He is a wide load barely being constrained by his cheap suit. A bulbous balloon head with beady eyes sits on top of his body and, sometimes, on top of the head sits a mangy toupee that resembles the ass-end of a lemur defecating in North Nowhere Fuckistan.

As news director (not to be confused with the hardworking director of a newscast) he runs the news department and sets the tone for what goes on the air. He is prone to shaping the news in his own image. He likes to fire popular meteorologists, promote mediocre reporters to anchors and tends to call a riot an insurrection.

His assistant is Nan Carpy, frequently called 'Carpy the Harpy' behind her back. She is a shrieking mess of a human being from her unwashed rat's nest hair to her soulless black eyes to her wrinkled top with the faded OBAMA button pinned over her heart, to her baggy faded slacks to her open-toed shoes that reveal her nasty unkept digits. She frequently compliments Biff on his hair and loves to hate Mark Right and Steve Love.

"Hold it you two," Biff bellows toward Mark and

Steve, "word is that Burley Dick has a special job for both of you, so he has called in part-timers to work your jobs on the news tonight. This does not make me unhappy at all."

"Yeah creeps," Nan screams, "the part-timers will do a much better job."

Mark looks at Steve. "We're going to get dicked."

"Watch your filthy mouth," Nan shouts.

Mark explains to Nan, "When Burley Dick has a special job for you that's called getting dicked."

"Not something you would know about," Steve adds.

Nan explodes, "I know plenty, and I know you two jerks are always looking at my ass."

"Steve, are we looking at Nan's ass?" Mark asks.

"No, Mark, we look at women's asses, and I don't think she's a woman."

"Creeps! Perverts! Hacks!" Nan is shaking with delirium.

Mark feigns a somber tone. "That hurts. You called us hacks." He pushes the down button, the elevator door opens, and Steve and he step in as Carpy continues her tirade.

"Cretins! Nutjobs! Neanderthals! Boss, you need to fire them right now! They should be working at a carwash."

"Nan, they don't work for me."

"They will soon. I write a letter to the owner every

day. I tell him how great you are and how incompetent Veal is and how he should make you the general manager."

"Thanks, Nan."

"When you become general manager, you can fire anybody."

They enter the breakroom.

"Boss, your hair looks great today."

"Thanks, Nan."

CHAPTER 2
I Hate That Bitch

Spring 1923
The Union of Soviet Socialist Republics
The Countryside near Gori, Georgia

A man stands outside a ramshackle hovel. Perhaps it was once a home or a barn or a school or a whorehouse, or maybe all four. The man is vigorously smoking a sleek, black pipe. He wears a tidy, gray, military-style uniform with no emblems or insignias. He has black boots and a black leather cap. Holstered to his right hip is a Nagant Model 1895 single-action revolver. It holds seven rounds of 7.62 mm ammunition.

This man is Joseph Stalin. He was born in Gori as Ioseb Besariones Dzejughashvil. Stalin is the latest and last of the nearly thirty names he has used. The historical record of today shows him as a seminary student (really), choirboy (really), poet, meteorologist in an observatory, labor organizer, newspaper editor, gangster, terrorist, extortionist, employee of the Rothschilds (Hmmm…), torcher of the Rothschild facility where he worked (Maybe), failed revolutionary, prisoner, person in exile, escapee-in-drag (really), robber, assassin, successful revolutionary, ruthless dictator, mass murderer and cultivator of one of history's greatest moustaches.

On this day he is a Bolshevik and chairman of the central committee of the communist party in the brand-new U.S.S.R. Vladimir Lenin is in charge in Moscow, but he is in very poor health. Leon Trotsky is to be his successor. Stalin has other plans. He puts out his pipe, stashes it in his pocket, and enters the building through a very creaky door. He has come to his home area to recruit a personal cadre, a security detail that answers only to him. He walks to the head of the room and stares at the twenty-five men gathered there. They are wearing faded and ill-fitted versions of Stalin's own uniform. Many of them have holes in their boots. Some of them have personal knives or pistols. Most of this rough crew has some degree of facial hair and a malnourished look. Stalin has issued each of them a M1891 Mosin rifle 7.62 mm. The rifles are very used having seen action during Russia's humiliation in the recent great war. But even though they are scratched and dented, the guns are still formidable weapons.

One of the men has a bulge in his pants but it is not because of his excitement at seeing Stalin. It is from a Nagant stick grenade that he has stuffed in his pocket. He found the grenade in the woods near his home when he went there to look for a cute wild boar. He plans on impressing Stalin by using the grenade in battle, but things don't always work out.

Stalin steps behind a crooked lectern at the head of the room and starts to address the group, "Men you are the ones of luck. You have been chosen to protect me, Stalin!" The men cheer. "I have removed the filthy ass of the Tsar from his throne. I have defeated the Mensheviks! I have cut off the dicks of the armies that tried to stop our revolution! I am Stalin, the mighty ass of Bolshevism!"

As the men applaud, the cabin door opens and a man in an out of place tweed suit and vest walks in. This man is Leon Trotsky. He was born Lev Davidovich Bronstein and is Stalin's fellow revolutionary. Trotsky is the intellectual thug to Stalin's brutal thug. He has bad hair, bad eyes, and bad ideas. His current title is People's Commissar of Military and Naval Affairs of the Soviet Union. He is destined to become one of history's biggest losers, pretty much at the hands of Stalin. He has been sent by Lenin to keep an eye on Stalin. Despite his entrance, Stalin continues speaking.

"Now I will take on the infidel that is the western

dog. I learn his language good and teach it to you so that we may ingrate ourselves into his spherical influence. We will talk like the infidel. We will plant ourselves into him. We will cut his throat. We will use his women to pull our plows."

"Comrade Stalin," Trotsky interrupts. "While standing outside I could hear you praising yourself and leaving out our beloved Lenin."

"Men, this is our sneakable commissar who has been to New York. He will tell us of the corruption. Speak Bronstein."

"I am now known as Leon Trotsky."

"Ulyanov becomes Lenin. I become Stalin, man of steel. You become Trotsky? How inspiring of awe."

"It means man stronger than steel."

"It means man who runs to shit."

The men erupt in raucous laughter. Trotsky fumes and emits an ill-advised retort.

"Well ... you pass gas in your sleep."

"How do you know, Bronstein? How do you know?"

Stalin laughs at Trotsky then speaks to the group, "Men, the revolution will become untidy if it is burdened up with names. From now on each of you will be known as Sergei."

"But steel one," a man speaks up. "Each of us is already known as Sergei."

"This country needs more names," Trotsky

mumbles to himself.

"I am not Sergei," speaks another man. "I am Ivan."

"Then, Ivan, you will be my sergeant and will lead these soldiers to my glorification."

"Thank you, mighty ass."

"Bronstein! Speak of the west."

Trotsky collects himself and steps behind the lectern. "Gentlemen, I have seen the west. They live fast. They have money. They have things." Various men respond.

"They have things."

"They have money."

"They have fast."

"I wish we have things," Ivan says.

"Yes, they have things," Trotsky continues. "But we should not be afraid of these things."

Stalin jumps in, "We have no need of things. We have the revolution!"

"Glory to the revolution," the men respond.

"You have the revolution," Stalin murmurs to himself. "I will have things." He shifts his focus back to the men. "The education continues now at this moment." He picks up a dried cow chip from the floor and begins writing on the wall. Trotsky takes notice.

"What in Dante's sweet Hell are you writing with?"

Stalin waves the chip at him. "This is the quite useful stuff that comes from the beautiful ass of your girlfriend, Bronstein."

"Oy-vai," Trotsky is shaken. "This culture has a long way to go."

Stalin writes for a while picking up more cow chips as needed. Finally, he is ready to address the group. "Men, we will need to learn phrases like these as we prepare to defeat the west. Repeat after me."

"Repeat after me," the men eagerly respond.

"Not yet."

"Not yet."

"Just wait,' Stalin yells.

"Just wait."

Stalin emphatically points at the first phrase on the wall. "Nice to see you commodore Vanderbilt. Please pass the veal."

"Nice to see you commodore Vanderbilt. Please pass the veal."

"He is dead," Trotsky tries to point out, but Stalin proceeds.

"May I drive your automobile, Mr. Ford?"

"May I drive your automobile, Mr. Ford?"

"Most of these men could not even drive a farm wagon," Trotsky tries to no avail. Stalin moves on.

"Hello, President Roosevelt. Is that a trust in your pants or are you just busting out to see me?"

"Hello, President Roosevelt. Is that a trust in your pants or are you just busting out to see me?"

"He is dead, too, and that makes no damned sense!" Trotsky is beside himself.

There is a knock at the door. This disturbs Stalin, and he opens the door in a bad humor. A dreary, old peasant woman steps in carrying a basket of dried pork. She takes a long look around the room then addresses Stalin in a local dialect which translates something like this:

"Soso, the men are very handsome and smell so nice."

"What do you want, babushka? I told you not to come here and not to call me that."

"I bring pork for the men. Pork for the revolution!"

"Pork! Pork! Pork!" the Sergeis and Ivan scream with delight.

The twenty-five swarm the woman and the pork is quickly devoured. Stalin is quite irate and bellows at her. "You have interrupted my lecture!" He pulls and cocks his pistol in one swift motion and fires a single shot into her forehead. She falls into a heap. He coldly stares at her body for a moment then issues an order, "Sergei! Bury my mother!" As he walks away, he speaks under his breath, "I hate that bitch!"

Present Day
WDOA

The elevator door creaks open and Mark and Steve step out into the unfinished basement of WDOA. They make a left turn and head toward a room in the southwest corner that is constructed of unpainted drywall. Mark steps up to the door and knocks three times under a sign that reads ALPHA CONTROL. They are beckoned to enter by a friendly voice and step inside.

Larry Biggsley sits behind an old Ampex editing console cutting one-inch video tape. He is the master control supervisor and chief editor at WDOA. This gives him the power to keep one-inch tape alive at the station as the one-time industry workhorse is now virtually obsolete. He is probably the last person in the country cutting one-inch tape by hand as that method was long ago replaced by computerized editing, which itself is now kaput, but Larry enjoys actually cutting the tape. And there is much exciting work to do these days as WDOA has just acquired the broadcast rights to his favorite *THE ANDY GRIFFITH SHOW* and Larry had all 249 episodes shipped in on one-inch tape. You would think it might be difficult for him to edit his favorite program, but there is one thing about the show that he does not like, as the clothesline strung around the room with strips of expunged tape attached by clothespins attests. More about that in a moment.

Larry is a large man but not overweight. He has a pleasant face and well-groomed dark hair. He is a couple of years younger than Mark and Steve but shares most of their sensibilities. He is wearing a button-down blue oxford short-sleeve shirt, cargo shorts, and white leather athletic shoes with no socks. He happily spins his chair around to greet Mark and Steve.

"Mark! Steve! Good to see you guys!"

"Hi Larry."

"Hiiiiiiiiiiiiii!" Steve sometimes likes to stretch out his "hi's" for comedic effect.

"Mark, sorry to hear about Moo."

"Thanks Larry. She was a great cat, and even though she never answered any of your messages, I know she thought a lot of you."

"Larry how are you doing now that the mall is open?" Steve interjects. It took your house and your whole neighborhood."

"Well ... Biggsley was going downhill, and my house was falling apart ... remember that joke I used to make about the tornado that went through Biggsley and did two million dollars in improvements?" Mark and Steve laugh at the memory. "Still, I miss my little house with that smelly Catgrass Creek in the backyard."

"And I hear the creek is still there," Mark points out. "It flows right through the south wing of the mall. Spooneybarger's way of getting past the EPA. And he deserves that stinking ditch."

Steve jumps in, "Your ancestors kicked Chief Don-ee-o's ass and took that land, right Larry?"

"Yeah ... that's the story, but my great, great, great whatever kind of ... just bought the place. The chief said the creek smelled like shit and he was being pestered by his dead ancestors, so he wanted to sell."

"How was he pestered by his dead ancestors?"

"Mark, you know about that."

"There's an old legend about that area. Something about being able to communicate with the departed ones in the orange glow of twilight. No cable show has ever pursued it, so who knows."

"Did you see any departed ones there Larry," Steve is curious.

"I saw my grandfather on the front porch once."

"Wow."

"He wasn't dead though. He had just escaped from the nursing home."

"So, Larry, what did your ancestor pay for the place?" Mark wants to know.

"It cost him four horses, three goats, a knife, an ax, and a prepaid visit for the chief from Lewisburg's top whore."

"Lewisburg had a whorehouse early on," Mark states.

"And this whore was an Indian, too. She was an Arapi-HO!" (They all laugh.)

"At least your new house on the east end is pretty nice," Steve says.

"It's not bad and it is fun to fuck with my new libtard neighbors. They said my '67 Chevy wagon was too rusty, so I had it painted lime green. Now they on the menu that day.

"Lunch came. I went through the line, got my food, and there were the beans. Garmon and I sat down together ate the rest of our food and looked at the beans. I really wanted that extra cake, so as Garmon watched, I went for it. Bite of beans. Drink of chocolate milk. Another bite. Another drink and, eventually, I got them down. Garmon looked at me, laughed and opened the top of his empty milk carton. He picked up his fork, shoveled his beans into the carton, and mashed down the top. I thought it was brilliant, but I never would have tried it.

"With that we went to show off our clean trays and get more cake. I stepped up to the counter first, was praised for cleaning my tray, and received my cake. I walked away, and Garmon stepped up. After sitting down, I looked back, and saw Garmon staring at me with a face full of hatred. Somehow, the lunch ladies had found his beans. He was busted. He blamed me, of course, but as God is my witness, I did not rat him out. Things were never the same between us after that day."

Steve laughs. "We used to have those beans at our school. We just said they were worms and threw them at the girls."

Mark is impressed. "That's pretty good. Wish I had thought of that."

Then Larry remembers something. "Guys, we've

been sitting here talking about the stupid mall and word is Dick is going to send you out there today to work with the 'great' J. P. Forte." Mark and Steve groan at the thought. "Burley thinks J. P. Forte hung the moon."

"I thought it was Neil Armstrong who did that," Mark says. "Ehhh… J. P. Forte, the famous A-list director who is all reputation and no talent."

"What's the name of that idiot that works with him?" Steve asks.

Larry laughs as Mark answers. "They call him Hotwad. Hoddington Wadsworth the Fifth. He's almost seven feet tall and can't play a lick of basketball. His father got him into three different ivy league schools, and he flunked out of all three. Now he pushes a portable trophy case around with all of Forte's awards. Local video awards are all a scam, and I really think Forte bought his regional Emmy off eBay."

Steve looks at a piece of tape that is hanging near his head. "That's Aunt Bea," Larry tells him.

"Oh, yeah. We've got Andy Griffith now. I guess you have to cut for commercials."

"I cut because of Aunt Bea." He gestures at the pieces of tape hanging around the room. "They're all Aunt Bea. I'm cutting her out. I hate that bitch."

"I thought it was your favorite show."

"I love it. The greatest TV show of all time. I even

like the color ones."

"But ... Aunt Bea..."

"Bitch."

Mark jumps in, "If you're talking bitches, don't forget Helen Crump. Geez. Colder than the Wasilla, Alaska, Dairy Queen in January. I wish Mary the nurse had stayed on as Andy's girlfriend; she even had a Thunderbird Sport Roadster, but I'm sure Joanna Moore was much more expensive than Aneta Corsaut."

Steve is shaken but goes on, "Well, Larry, you can't cut her out of the pickle episode."

"I hate the pickle episode." Larry picks up a plastic case. "Here it is, and I'm going to misplace it."

Steve stands in stunned silence as Mark tries to pick up the slack, "Steve, Larry and I have discussed the pickle episode during our late-night phone calls, and we think a lot of it is stupid like the way Barney gets rid of the pickles. I mean handing them out to passing motorists, he should have just dumped them in a ditch."

Steve then decides to bring up a memory that may massage the situation, "I had a dream about Aunt Bea once." Larry and Mark stare at him with a mixture of puzzlement and curiosity. "It's the middle of the night ... I wake up and see an apparition at the foot of my bed. It's blurry at first but then it becomes clearer—it's Aunt Bea. She has a big grin on her face.

Then, she starts unbuttoning her blouse…she goes very slowly and finally takes it off. Next, she unhooks her bra and tosses it on my bed as two huge melons pop out. She grins even more as she fondles herself and finally, she says, 'Steve, do you like what you see?' I say, 'why yes. Yes, I do.' Then I wake up and realize it's a dream, and I'm glad because how could I like that?"

There is a moment of silence, then the three of them burst out laughing. Their moment of merriment is ruined, as it usually is, when the voice of Burley Dick bellows out of the overhead speaker, "Steve Love and Mark Right to the production office. Steve Love and Mark Right to the production office. Now!"

Mark and Steve groan in unison as they turn toward the door. "Sorry guys," Larry consoles. "At least I warned you … oh … wait I forgot to tell you something. My last few years in Biggsley, the neighborhood was going downhill, so I hid some weapons around the backyard in case I ever got attacked while I was out there grilling."

"Good idea," Mark concurs as Steve nods in approval.

"When I moved, I forgot one thing. Right on the top of the creekbank where my backyard ended, I hid a nice, heavy metal Bowie knife under a big blue rock. Why don't you guys see if you can find it? It should be right in front of that Russian joint."

"Sure thing, *broheim*," Steve states as the two of them wave and exit.

Larry turns toward his edit console, "All right, bitch. Let's go another round."

CHAPTER 3
"Let Me Be Adamant About That"

Mark and Steve are traversing the long hallway toward Burley Dick's office. Steve is speculating on what mood Burley Dick will be in although, deep down, he already knows.

"I wonder if Dick is in an 'intoxicating' mood."

"People shouldn't drink this early," Mark responds.

"It's just his 'medication.'"

"I'd like to find a doctor to prescribe me that kind of medication." Mark makes a drinking motion with his thumb.

"Not on our health plan, roadie."

"With all the drunks around here, I think that is our health plan. Have a drink and you will feel better."

The pair reach Burley Dick's office and stand side-by-side in the open doorway waiting to be acknowledged. Burley sits behind his computer, struggling to operate it. He is middle-aged, middle management and of middling intelligence. Mark and Steve would easily best him in an IQ test.

Burley wears a white shirt with a starched collar, held tight by a red bow tie with white polka dots, an unbuttoned gray vest that his large gut protrudes from, and gray slacks that hang an inch too short over his spider legs. He is trying to channel a Jason Robards from *All the President's Men* vibe, but his look trends more toward clown school dropout or a Dagwood Bumstead impersonator. His small head of salt and pepper hair, slathered down by a Newsom-esque amount of grease, is matched by a scraggly beard sans moustache. He thinks this makes him look like Abraham Lincoln, but the only person he has ever freed is Steve Love, and he emancipated Mr. Love from being a brilliant videographer. He has beady eyes, a crooked nose that looks down at everyone, and tiny rhinoceros' ears. And yes, the Polestar 2 belongs to him.

He attended college at Illinois State University where he played cymbals in the marching band, although he never made the road squad. He was reluctant to pick a major, so he was assigned to television production. After college he spent some time in the Army where he saw no action but applied for a Purple Heart after a boiler explosion in his barracks caused him to crap his pants. This request was turned down.

TIME MALL

After the Army, he bounced around the Midwest as a television director, staying one step ahead of his mediocrity until he landed the production manager job at WDOA. He has no accomplishments at his current position but is believed to have once followed a female anchor, long since departed from the station, to a nearby gym for her lunchtime workout and stolen her leather pants from the locker room. The poor girl had to return to the station and anchor the 4:00 p.m. news in her gym shorts. If a plexiglass news desk had been in use that day, Channel 82 might have briefly climbed out of the ratings cellar as the broadcast went on and word got around about the sexy live legs.

Finally, Burley Dick turns and looks at Mark and Steve. Steve breaks the ice.

"Hi Dick!"

"That's Mr. Dick," Burley intones in his pseudo-authoritarian voice.

"Definitely."

Burley looks at Mark. "I see you managed to get him away from the coffee pot."

"It's not as strong as what you're drinking."

"I am on blood pressure medication because of my stressful job. Nothing more."

"Yes sir, Mr. Dick," Mark responds knowing the truth.

"FYI, I have a frustrating task for you two."

Steve jumps in. "More frustrating than the time you sent us to shoot that redneck who was having new windows installed in his house …?"

"…for that infomercial," Mark adds. "And we were lucky to get out of there before the banjos started playing."

"You should have stuck around longer. YAGT, you are going to—"

Mark interrupts. "The incredible new Taj Ma-Mall, the temple of commerce, to work with Mr. J.P. Forte, the Scorsese of industrials and sausage commercials."

"I suppose Biggsley told you. He thinks he knows everything, but he knows nothing."

"He never told us what we are going to shoot for Mr. Forte," Steve says as he pantomimes a camera on his shoulder.

"You are going to shoot nothing. Let me be adamant about that. Mr. Forte needs lights because his own lights are under quarantine at the sausage plant. You will take our new state-of-the-art LED lighting kits to him and assist in any way needed. Leave the old Fresnels here; I don't want Mr. Forte or his brilliant assistant Hotwad to risk getting burned."

"A light's not effective unless it gets hot enough to sear flesh," Steve states.

"So, what is Mr. Forte going to shoot?" Mark asks. Is Young Bucks Sausage going to slaughter some hogs out there?"

"Mr. Spooneybarger and Mr. Trafalgar have commissioned a calendar called The Girls of the Taj Ma-Mall." Steve starts to make incoherent noises. "Mr. Forte will shoot both the still shots for the calendar and the making of video as these young women pose in their swimsuits." Steve's mouth falls open and a blank stare overtakes his face. "What's the matter with him?"

"It's the pre-alimony stare. Calendar girls in bathing suits. You may be sending him out to meet a future ex-wife."

"Make him stop it. He's drooling on my carpet."

"Steve … Steve … divorce lawyer!"

"Huh … what … oh, hey bro. Thanks, I needed that. I thought Dick said we were going to see some calendar girls."

Burley Dick stands up and totters on his knobby ankles, trying to stretch out his six-foot-two frame in a weak attempt to menace. "Mr. Dick! And J.P. Forte will keep you two so busy you won't have time to look at anything." He walks over to Steve and points at his shirt. "By the way, blue oxford collared shirts and khaki pants are coming soon. I'm working on the memo now. And, Love, you should shave because your beard will never look like mine."

"Thank you, Jesus." Steve clutches his hands in prayer.

"Speaking of that, no more religious icons. I know you're still wearing that cross, Love."

Steve clutches his chest. "This is my faith, Mr. Dick."

Mark jumps in. "What about Nan Carpy and her Obama button?"

"That's not faith."

"It's her faith because she's an idiot."

Burley glowers. "Don't disparage your superiors. Even if they are female."

Mark shakes his head. "Khaki pants and blue oxford shirts, that's a big howdy. Are you also going to send us door-to-door to spread the good news about WDOA?"

"All male production personnel will wear Khaki pants and blue collared oxford shirts."

"What about female production personnel?" Mark adds. "Oh, that's right; you don't have any."

"Women have their place. Just not in my department. Now go pack up your lights and GOTR."

"Huh?" Steve looks puzzled.

"Get on the road!" Burley points toward the door.

"Why don't you just say that?" Mark asks.

"Get out!"

Mark and Steve exit as Steve nudges Mark with his elbow. "Bro, calendar girls!" Mark smiles as an announcement comes over the overhead speaker.

"Burley Dick, you have a call holding. Burley Dick, you have a call holding."

Mark pops back into Burley's office. "It's probably

from Holden Caulfield."

"O ... U ... T."

"What's that stand for?"

"Out!!!!!!!"

Mark disappears as Burley takes a small brown bottle from his upper left desk drawer and pours some of the contents into his coffee. "My blood pressure is OTCT, off the charts today." He takes a healthy sip then picks up the phone.

About an hour later, Steve and Mark head out of the WDOA parking lot and onto 7th Street. Steve is at the wheel of the aging, white Ford Econoline that belongs to the production department. Aboard are four cases of modern LED lights fabricated by Phantom Dynamics and a case of old 1K 'flesh burners,' assembled long ago by an out-of-business and forgotten manufacturer, that Steve brought along for fun. Mark unfolds a newspaper that he purloined from the breakroom.

"We should learn more about the mall and see what Garmon has us up against." He looks thru the paper. "Garmon Spooneybarger and Nelson Trafalgar present the Taj Ma-Mall where history meets commerce," he reads. "What a crock." Mark reads some more. "Shop at over 600 stores and interact with costumed characters who represent famous people from throughout time."

"This guy was really into history, huh?"

Mark bristles, "No! I was really into history. I always got A's in it. I won the school history award every year of high school. Garmon struggled with it but said it didn't matter because once he got rich, he would just buy history. We laughed at him but maybe he has done it."

"Did he build this mall just to bug you?" Steve wonders.

"It wouldn't surprise me. He was really upset about those beans." Mark reads on. "Here's some news about one of those costumed characters. It seems an actor dressed like a caveman made off with a vintage boombox from a store called 70s Nightmare. The thief emitted an extremely foul odor."

"Goddamned method actors."

"Them and clowns."

"Oooh," Steve has a moment of inspiration. "The worst of both worlds. A method acting clown."

"He would live in a house made out of elephant shit," Mark adds. Then Steve pipes in …

"And wipe his ass with cotton candy."

"I hate clowns," Mark resumes looking at the paper. "There's a gun store!"

"God bless America!"

"It's called It's Right to Bear Arms. And next to it is a tanning salon called It's Right to Bare Arms and So Much More."

"God bless tanning beds."

Mark gets very excited. "Wow, on display in the atrium is a Bell Rocket Belt from the 1960s. You know I've always called them jetpacks."

"Me, too, bro."

The problem with those was they could only carry 21 seconds worth of fuel.

"Wait a minute, dude. So, when John Robinson went looking for Penny and the Bloop that time he could not have flown around as long as he did?"

"Correct. He only had 21 seconds."

"They must have slowed down the film."

Mark smiles and paraphrases some more from the paper. "Here are some historic items on display in the gun store. Davy Crockett's rifle 'Old Betsy' is there. It's a 40-caliber flintlock custom made for him by a Mr. Graham from Franklin County, Kentucky. Also, Sergeant York's rifle from the First World War. A Springfield thirty-aught-six. And they have General Patton's helmet, riding crop, and field glasses."

"Bro! That is some sacred stuff! We'll have to stop and say a prayer."

"There's an Elvis store called The Gift of the Elvi."

"God bless the King."

"Here's some stuff about that Bolshevik store."

"God damn Russia."

"They have a Nagant machine gun from the Russian revolution complete with one box of ammo. That sounds like a bad idea. They have a crystal imperial eagle from Nicholas ll's personal collection. They have Stalin's pipe. It was found in Georgia …"

"Stalin went down to Georgia?"

"The country of Georgia."

"Oh, yeah. That one."

"He is believed to have lost the pipe there in 1923 while on a mission to recruit an elite personal guard. Hmm … I bet they were elite. And the pipe probably belonged to some old peasant woman."

"Yeah, Russians lie about everything."

"Here's some more Davy Crockett stuff. A Mexican restaurant called Taco Tormento has on display the diary of José Enrique de la Peña, who was a Mexican officer at the Alamo. In a diary entry just after the battle he claims to have witnessed Davy Crockett rise through the chapel roof into the air and fly off. What the hell is that about? Too much tequila? How could Davy Crockett rise into the air?"

"I think your answer is right there. Bad Mexican food."

Mark ponders the issue. "He killed a 'bar' when he was only three. You would think he could handle a tormented taco."

"No, bro. Daniel Boone killed a 'bar.' Davy killed a bear."

"You're right. D. Boone killed a 'bar' on this tree. Davy Crockett killed a bear when he was only three. Thanks Steve. I always get that mixed up."

Steve nods. "God, I love this country."

Mark returns to the newspaper. "'The atrium of the mall is one hundred feet tall covering an area the size of six football fields and is topped off by an onion dome. In the northeast corner sits a large English Manor house brought over piece-by-piece by Mr. Trafalgar from his home area of Richmond, England' … That's great, a fake person has a home area. 'The manor serves as a corporate headquarters for the mall and as the comfortable living quarters of Mr. Spooneybarger and Mr. Trafalgar.' I hope they are very happy together. 'Catgrass Creek flows out of the mile long, south wing and into the atrium terminating in a 20-foot waterfall that tumbles past the sub-atrium which sits 10 feet below. The water then travels 10 more feet into a sparkling collection pool.' … and then into the sewer system I bet. 'The west wing is a quarter mile long, features many restaurants and is also accessible to food trucks. The east wing, also a quarter mile long, contains a nine-hole golf course and will eventually house an amusement park' … Spooneybarger hasn't even finished the place yet."

"There is a 20-screen movie theatre. The restrooms feature marble floors and gold faucets. There are over 7,000 employees, and Spooney is screwing over every one of them. Here's something interesting. A holographic photo booth. You can have your picture taken with anyone from history. That could be good.

Steve, my friend, you are going to have your picture taken with Lady Godiva, and I am going to be adamant about that."

"Woo-hoo! Let's get to that there mall!" Steve mashes the gas pedal.

CHAPTER 4
Talking While Riding On A Special Flotation Chassis

Steve and Mark are still headed toward the Taj Ma-Mall, which is several miles away. They are quiet now. Mark is thinking about his life and wonders if he has really accomplished anything. He worries that he is just an annoying history know-it-all spouting facts that no one wants to hear. Steve is thinking about women doing housework in their underwear. Suddenly, the van hits a pothole and bounces violently which elicits a loud "Fuck!" from Mark and an explanation from Steve.

"Burley Dick says this van has a special flotation chassis to protect the delicate equipment that we haul around."

"Burley Dick is a lying sack of shit," Mark responds. "The shocks are worn out and he's too cheap to get them replaced." Mark turns on the radio and hears: "The Crowe Furniture Company. Give us a caw." He quickly turns the radio off which gets Steve's attention.

"Dude, you wrote that."

"I'm not proud," Mark fumes. "Those cheap bastards at Crowe dub the audio off their TV spots that I wrote and get free radio commercials."

"At least you've done something. They won't let me do anything. I wouldn't even mind shooting a sausage commercial.

"That would piss Forte off for sure," Mark laughs.

"I know." Steve smiles then thinks of something. "Don't you want to write a movie script? You should do that."

"I want to do that. I just can't come up with a story idea. A great plot that would blow people away. I know the kind of movie it would be, an action comedy about two buddies facing dire consequences, but what are the consequences?"

"I guess it's hard to come up with something like that."

"And the dialogue must be good. Let's say the two guys are driving around discussing important back-story points. It would have to be interesting, or the audience would tune out."

"Hmm."

"Uh-huh."

"Yep."

"Heh."

Steve suddenly has a thought. "Maybe the two guys could stop at a red light and a blonde with big tits could walk in front of them."

"Tits are good. I'm going to have some in my movie. I just need that one can't-miss idea and I can tell Burley Dick to kiss my ass."

"I wouldn't want his lips on my ass, roadie."

"Yeah, I would probably get alcohol poisoning through osmosis." Mark thinks for a moment and groans as the van hits another pothole. "I just need to come up with my own *Citizen Kane*."

"Maybe your standards are too high, bro. People call *The Waterboy* Adam Sandler's *Citizen Kane*."

"I thought it was *Happy Gilmore*."

"I guess *Citizen Kane* is alright, but for a great movie it's hard to beat *Goldfinger*."

Mark gets excited. "I love *Goldfinger*. Hell yeah. You didn't see any bikini babes hanging out with Charles Foster Kane. He thought that weird singer-bitch was attractive."

"She was nasty," Steve gags.

Mark affects a Sean Connery accent. "Pussy, I'd like you to meet Mr. Kane."

"That's pretty good, and don't forget James Bond had that great Aston Martin, Kane just had a stupid sled."

"I just need to come up with my own personal

Goldfinger."

"Maybe you could base the two buddies on you and me," Steve is excited at the thought.

"Who would get cast as us."

"As long as Seth Rogan doesn't play me, I don't care." Steve stops the van at a red light. A shapely blonde with enormous breasts held hostage in a spandex prison traverses the crosswalk in front of them. "I'd like to milk those and make porno ice cream."

"It's a shame our generation was bottle fed," Mark rues.

1923
The Countryside Near Gori, Georgia

Stalin and his Bolsheviks are creaking through the dreary countryside on a well-worn wooden wagon drawn by a pair of mangy oxen. Ivan, who can drive a farm wagon, is at the reins. While back at the shack, he had embraced his promotion by picking up a cow chip and drawing sergeant stripes on his shoulders. Stalin sits to his right. The 24 Sergeis are packed into the back like Black Sea sardines. Trotsky barely clings to the lowered tailgate. Suddenly the wagon hits a pothole and bounces violently which elicits a loud "Fuck!" from Stalin and an explanation from Ivan.

"My uncle build this wagon himself. He install

special flotation chassis to protect deliberate equipment that we haul around."

"Your uncle lies in a sack of shit. This pile is all junk. Your uncle must be a kulak. I will hang him soon."

In the back of the wagon the Sergeis have been peppering Trotsky with inane questions about farm animals. Now one of them asks about an earlier revolution attempt.

"Great Commissar Trotsky. What was it like during the first revolution?"

"1905. It was small. It was a struggle. There were challenges." Trotsky begins to think back.

1905
The Russian Hinterlands

Lenin is standing on a wooden platform speaking to a small crowd. Stalin and Trotsky are seated to his right on rickety wooden crates. His speech has reached its climax.

"My people, there is one more thing I must ask of you. If you truly believe in the revolution. If you truly believe in the evil of the bourgeois elite. If you truly believe that the Tsar must be removed. If you truly believe that I am the man to lead you to greatness. Then you must drop your pants for Bolshevism!" The onlookers stare in stunned silence.

"I said you must drop your pants for Bolshevism!" Lenin steps forward and unfastens his pants, they fall to his ankles to reveal that he is wearing red boxer shorts with little yellow hammers and sickles all over them. The small crowd cheers as the men join in and drop their pants. Most of them are not wearing underwear. The couple of women in the crowd laugh and giggle.

Now Lenin looks at Trotsky who dutifully stands up and reveals that he has gotten the boxer memo. There are more cheers and then it is Stalin's turn, and he quickly shows that he is a member of the no underwear group as his own grotesque, hairy member faces the gallery. He promptly starts shaking it at them and loud cheers erupt, even from the women. Trotsky pulls up his pants, sits down and buries his face in his hands as the crate collapses beneath him. The crowd and Stalin roar with laughter and even the dour Lenin emits a chuckle. Trotsky can only mutter a pathetic "Oy-vai."

1923

Trotsky cringes at the memory. "There were certain reasons that the first revolution was unsuccessful."

Stalin suddenly orders Ivan to stop the wagon. He jumps down and starts undoing his pants as he disappears behind a clump of nearby bushes, this is not to support Bolshevism but to answer a sudden urge. The Sergeis pile out of the wagon and stand attentively anticipating an order that is imminent. A few minutes later Stalin's hand pushes through a bush and the order is issued. "Oak leaves! Bring me oak leaves to wipe the mighty ass of Bolshevism!"

Stalin has adopted the classic notion that oak leaves equal strength and only they can clean him after evacuation. While there are a variety of oak trees in Georgia, most of Stalin's new crew could not identify one and it is also early spring and no leaves are fully emerged so the Sergeis run around, like Curly impersonators at a *Three Stooges* convention, collecting various dead leaves from the ground and delivering them to their leader's hand. Eventually Stalin is satisfied and emerges with a plan, "Now let us find somebody to kill."

Present Day

Mark and Steve are continuing their trip when Steve spots a UPS truck and gives it the finger. Mark understands completely. "UPS. That was your first wife, right?"

"Yep, the first one," Steve thinks back.

22 Years Earlier

Steve enters his house and notices a clipboard and package on his kitchen table. He looks around and finds a UPS uniform on the floor entangled with his wife's clothing. "No! Damn you UPS!"

Present Day

"Then there was number two. Hmm … number two. Sounds about right."

Eleven Years Earlier

Steve enters his house and notices a clipboard and package on the kitchen table. He looks around and finds a FedEx uniform on the floor entangled with his wife's clothing. "No! Damn you Federal Express!"

Present Day

"Number three had lower standards."

Six Years Earlier

Steve enters his house and notices a mailbag on the kitchen table. He looks around and finds a postal uniform on the floor entangled with his wife's clothing.

"No! Damn you United States Postal Service!"

Present Day

Mark weighs in. "UPS and Federal Express are one thing, but losing one to the mailman …"

"I know. And I always left him a Christmas present. But number four was the toughest."

Two Years Earlier

Steve enters his house and notices a 'Happy Birthday' balloon tied to a kitchen chair. He looks around and finds a clown suit on the floor entangled with his wife's clothing. "No! Damn you Big Top Delivery Service!"

Present Day

"And the bastard was delivering the balloon for my birthday. I hate clowns."

"It should be legal to kill them," Mark proclaims.

1923

Stalin has led his men on a trek a few hundred yards from the wagon. He spots a barely standing structure ahead and issues an order. "Men. Our target approaches. Conspire to attack!"

Trotsky senses the developing disaster and tries to intervene. "That is a residence for chickens."

Stalin does not care and issues the attack order. The Sergeis charge the coop with guns a-blazing. They run in and out of both doors at random. There is loud screaming from both Russians and chickens as flying feathers fill the air. Eggs start breaking and feathers start sticking to the Sergeis. Some Sergeis emerge with an attacking chicken on their head as Stalin yells encouragement. "Fight, you bastards! Fight those peckers!"

The chickens put up a brave fight. Pecking. Scratching. Defecating. The Sergeis are bloody and fouled by the fowl, but eventually the voice of the cluckers grows silent and the foul Bolsheviks secure the coop. Stalin proclaims victory, "The bourgeois feather mongers have been defeated!"

Then an old peasant woman runs from a nearby hovel screaming in a fractured dialect which translates as, "Fuck Bolsheviks! Fuck Bolsheviks! Fuck Bolsheviks!"

Enraged, Stalin decides to test Ivan. "Sergeant, your mighty ass is under attack. Act now perhaps."

The excited Ivan calls out the orders. "Ready! Aim! Fire!" All 24 Sergeis discharge their weapons into the doomed babushka who plops to the ground with a sickening sound. Stalin stares down at her.

"Flinty mouthed kulak, she whores the chickens for herself when the revolution desires them."

A shaken Trotsky tries to speak. "We have just engaged a house of chickens and shot an old woman. This is not the people's revolution." Stalin whispers into Ivan's ear. A moment later an egg hits Trotsky in the face. It is quickly followed by several more. He takes off his glasses and tries to shake the yolk off. "How inspiring."

Present Day

As the van rolls on Steve spots the atrium of the Taj Ma-Mall off in the distance. "Thar she blows!"

"There's that onion dome. Really Spooney." Mark's disdain is starting to heat up.

"So," Steve winds up a fat pitch. "Besides the green beans and the English and Russian stuff and the mall. Are there any other reasons you hate this guy?"

"He stole my prom date. Then he married her and murdered her."

"Whoa! Your girlfriend?"

Not really my girlfriend. Boy, this is going to be hard to talk about. Beth Marie Shoreham was the class of our class. She was a fine woman among girls. She had a compact pleasing figure. Pleasant smile. Bright hazel eyes. Silky black hair in a Dorothy Hamill haircut. She could cook. She could play the piano.

She liked beer. She had a sweet fifteen-foot jump shot. And even though she was from Indianapolis, she had a charming southern accent. The perfect woman."

"Wow."

"She didn't believe in high school romances. Thought they were a waste of time. But some lucky guys could get a dinner date now and then. I never quite made that cut, but we were friendly toward each other. Sometimes I would walk by her and make a joke. One time she was eating in that smelly cafeteria, and I walked by her and said, 'They just found Jimmy Hoffa. Don't touch the meatloaf.'"

"That's funny." Steve laughs.

"I did make her card once at a school dance. Yes, she had a dance card. We danced to 'Shout' and really went at it. I was moving so well I told her I got my shoes from the Fred Astaire estate settlement. The best ad-lib I ever made. When most people hear 'Shout' they think of John Belushi. I think of Beth Marie Shoreham.

"As senior prom approached, she decided to hold a raffle to pick her prom date. The proceeds would go to help homeless cats. I was not as into cats as much then as I am now, but it seemed like a nice cause. Guys bought tickets like crazy. Garmon bought a bunch and expected victory. I took a shitty part-time job at the local Stuckey's so I could buy more tickets. When the winner was announced, I was stunned to find out it was me. Wow." Mark uses his right index finger to wipe a tear from the corner of his right eye. "I quit my job at Stuckey's and started preparing for the prom. Finally, the night arrived."

31 Years Earlier

Mark is ready to leave for the prom but has just enough time to step in the bathroom and admire himself again. He sets Beth Marie's corsage down and stares into the mirror. He loves the fluffy haired young man in the mauve tuxedo staring back at him and gives himself a thumbs up. He steps over to the toilet, unzips, and does his business. As he flushes a golden retriever pushes thru the slightly ajar bathroom door and heads to the toilet.

"Dad! Get the dog out of here!"

Mark's father yells from the living room. "She needs a drink. She was out playing with Ceep. Her bowls empty."

"Fill up the bowl!"

"Can't. The games on. Let her get a drink."

Mark and the thirsty mutt jockey for position around the toilet. As he attempts to zip up, the dog's tail is caught in his fly. Realizing her tail is in jeopardy the bitch becomes a beast.

"No! Dad! Help!"

"Let her get a drink."

Present Day

Mark sighs. "I was severely mauled in a vital area."

"I can see why you like cats now, bro."

"After I laid on the floor in pain awhile, the game finally hit half time, so dad called the paramedics. As I was being loaded on the gurney, I told dad to call Beth Marie and tell her what happened. By this time, the second half had started so he said he would call after the game. The game went into double overtime, so he never called."

"While being carted out the front door with Beth Marie's corsage clutched in my hands Garmon ran up. He just lived a few doors away and heard the commotion. I handed him the corsage and told him to tell Beth Marie what happened and to take her to the prom."

"Did he have a date?"

"He had hired an escort for the night, so he paid her off, put on his Nelson outfit and took Beth Marie. Then he told her I had ran off and joined the Peruvian navy."

"She believed that?"

"I don't know. I was away for a few weeks doing painful rehab. Finally, everything worked again, not that I needed to use it, and I returned shortly before graduation. I tried to tell her the dog story, but she didn't buy it thinking it was one of my jokes. She offered to refund my raffle money, but I told her the cats needed it more than me. Then she told me to call when I made admiral, saluted me, and walked off.

"After graduation she enrolled in a one-year course at a business college over on Hardtown Road."

"My sister went there for a while."

"Despite not being an admiral, I would call her now and then. She would talk for a couple of minutes then she would say she had to wash her hair. I heard that Garmon was calling her too. Sometimes as himself. Sometimes as Nelson. When she graduated, he had his dad hire her as an executive assistant. Now he had access to her every day.

"A couple of years went by, and we were all turning 21. Garmon's dad thought that was a good time to turn the company over to his son. That and he was worried about being indicted for that apartment building that collapsed in the west end."

"I remember that. What a mess."

"Ironically, Spooney's dad did flee to Peru. I guess Beth Marie was impressed that Garmon was now in charge. So, a few months later they got married. I was not invited. I thought about showing up outside the church like Dustin Hoffman, but I stayed home with a 12-pack of Coors, which had just become available in Hanktown. Why do women always go for the bad guy?"

"Dude, you'd have to watch Lifetime and Hallmark

24 hours a day for a month to even begin to understand that, and if you watched it that much you would want to blow your brains out."

"After they were married quite a while, the company was in bad shape. This was because of legal issues and Garmon's incompetence as a manager. Anyway, he needed cash, so he took out a two-million-dollar life insurance policy on Beth Marie. He also took a policy out on himself to provide cover. Then he bought her a brand-new Range Rover SUV. Told her it was the safest vehicle around and that he never wanted to collect on that policy. He really needed that money so just a few weeks later as Beth Marie was coming down Hollister Hill outside of town one evening the brakes failed." Mark pauses for 44 seconds. "A bright light went out."

"I'm sorry." Steve pauses for 27 seconds. "I don't want to sound cold, but this thing sounds like an episode of *Perry Mason*."

"Steve, do we watch too much MeTV?"

"Yes, Mark, we do. Hey! Maybe this Beth Marie story could be your movie."

"I could never write about that. Anyway, an investigation was inconclusive and Garmon Spooneybarger got his cash. Spooneybarger Construction was rebranded as Trafalgar Properties. And somehow, with the help of Nelson Trafalgar, Garmon Spooneybarger became a success. And here we are at his damned mall."

Steve steers the van into the huge parking lot of the Taj Ma-Mall. "It's big, broheim."

"That much is certain. Let's go in, congratulate Spooney then kick him in the nuts."

"Fuckin'-a, Bubba."

Mark and Steve's day is about to get a lot more interesting.

CHAPTER 5
The Temple of Commerce

On the southern tip of the south wing of the Taj Ma-Mall sits the holographic photo booth. It is certainly not a booth but a rather large room although it seems tucked into the mall's infrastructure as an afterthought as it sits between a food storage warehouse for the mall's restaurants on its right and a service entrance on its left. The service entrance, tucked between the photo booth and the creek, is accessed by a narrow foot path. This is the point where Catgrass Creek gurgles into the building via a special aqueduct system. The west bank promenade ends at the creek. On the east side the promenade continues to the photo booth. There is a footbridge across the creek at this spot. The closest public entrance is nearly 200 yards away at the 20-screen cinema.

At this moment, the booth is getting its latest customer as a diminutive man enters and approaches the young, white coated, bespectacled techie type sitting behind a large control panel in front of a bank of computers on the east side of the room. "Young man have I landed at the point where I may discover a photograph of myself and Mr. Christopher Columbus?"

"Sir? Oh … yes, I can take your picture with Columbus, and please call me Nate."

"I know he is not well thought of today, and I find that sad. I am from the Italian-American society of Lewisburg, and he is still a hero to us. He was so brave."

"We make no judgements, sir, just profits," states Nate as he types, pushes buttons, and manipulates levers. A couple of his movements are real, but most are for show, as consultants have suggested that it is what the customers would expect. "Please look to your right, sir." He points to the other end of the room where a large, golden proscenium arch stretches over a highly polished, slightly elevated steel stage painted to resemble wood. A crystal chandelier hangs in front of the arch. At the request of Garmon Spooneybarger the setup was built to resemble the Bolshoi in Moscow.

The space inside the arch fills with flashing lights as a slight whirring sound commences. It is quite an illuminated show. Then the chandelier starts to glow orange as Nate shakes his head. "That orange light is not in the program. It keeps showing up, and I can't figure out where it's coming from."

Suddenly Christopher Columbus appears standing on the aft deck of the Santa Maria. The customer is beside himself.

"It's him! It's him! Oh, he is so handsome!"

"Step right over there, sir, and up on the stage. Please use the handrail."

Despite his shaking knees the man makes his way up the three stairs on the left side of the stage and stands beside the great explorer. "He is looking right at me!"

"It's a very realistic program, sir."

The man places his arm around Columbus' shoulder as Nate works more buttons and levers. Finally, an eight-by-ten color glossy slides out of a slot in the computer behind the performance techster. Nate grabs the print and slides it into a clear plastic sleeve. "You may step down now, sir." The customer does so and approaches the control console with a smile on his face.

"I could see the ocean up there. I could feel the movement of the ship!"

Nate hands the man his picture. "That's what we strive for. That will be $17.95."

"Quite a bargain," states the pleased man as he hands over a credit card. The transaction is completed, and as the satisfied purchaser approaches the exit he looks back and notices Columbus is still on stage. "How long does he stay there?"

"We leave the current image up for a bit. It helps attract customers. And buried on the south end like we are we don't get as many people in here as one might expect. I think we should be near the main entrance."

"I agree. More people would discover you there." The man exits. Nate checks his computers for a couple of minutes then sets up a very low-tech sign that reads "BACK IN 15 MINUTES". He then enters a back room and closes the door behind him. A few minutes later, Christopher Columbus shakes his head and steps down from the stage. He is befuddled, but his natural curiosity compels him to explore the strange room. He looks, touches, smells, and eventually leaves the room and enters the new world of the Taj Ma-Mall. Nate reenters the room, takes down his sign and notices the deck of the Santa Maria without Columbus. "Now where did he go? That mass murderer should still be there. This keeps happening. I better run some more diagnostics." He pushes a button, and the Santa Maria disappears in 10 seconds.

Over a mile away at the main entrance Mark and Steve, having unloaded and parked the van, approach the steel and stone façade. Mark advances to the farthest right of the two dozen doors and holds it open for Steve who pushes thru a four wheeled cart with the five black cases of lights. Once inside, they stop to look around and take it all in. The onion dome high above them with its donut shaped observation deck allowing a panoramic look out at Lewisburg or a look down, over a double pipe safety rail, into the atrium. It is accessed by a glass encased elevator. The manor house to their left with the green of the golf course just beyond that. The food trucks and kiosks off to their right. The south wing stretching off into a mercantile infinity. The sound and smell of the 20-foot wide Catgrass Creek, flanked on each side by a 25-foot promenade, as it flows into the southern edge of the atrium and becomes the 20-foot waterfall. Young women walking around in shorts that are barely there. Costumed actors annoying the throngs of shoppers.

Mark hates the feeling, but he is somewhat overwhelmed and is compelled to make a pronouncement, "In Xanadu did Garmon Spooneybarger a stately commerce dome decree." He then glances back at the entry doors and notices something curious. "Look Steve, thick steel plates are hanging above all the doors on some kind of mechanism. I think Spooney can seal this place off if he wants to."

"Is this guy fuckin' Blofeld or something?"

"He probably thinks he is."

"Don't you think that was messed up with the good Bond movies. Blofeld was supposed to be the same guy, but he was always different."

"Yeah," Mark concurs. "Donald Pleasance was

too weird. Telly Savalas was too jerky, and Charles Gray was too fruity."

"Maybe Orson Welles should have done it."

"Mr. Kane as Mr. Blofeld. Hmmm. That's pretty good, Steve. Orson was great in that crazy 'Casino Royale' movie with David Niven." Mark takes a moment to ponder all things Bond. "Just don't get me started on all the Felix Leiters."

Suddenly, a crewman from the *Titanic* runs by shouting. "Iceberg! Dead ahead! Iceberg Dead ahead!"

"Another method actor," Mark scoffs. "He probably slept in a freezer last night to prepare."

"Look at that one." Steve points to a medieval type drawing away on a large sketchpad. "Hey! Michelangelo! What's up dude?"

The sketcher turns and glares at Steve. "Leonardo! Leonardo!"

Steve looks at Mark. "I always get those two mixed up."

Having made good time from the southern tip of the mall, Columbus walks by Mark and Steve looking lost and confused. "Hey! Columbus is lost," says Mark. "At least the guy is putting something into the role. I must admit, method or not, the actors are better than I expected." He notices an actor dressed as Abraham Lincoln approaching a group of young women. "But I think that's about to change." Mark recognizes the guy from bad local spots, including his own for Crowe's Furniture. The pathetic thespian has a vast C-list resume, but he has still not met his personal goal of snagging a 'Young Bucks' sausage commercial.

The girls giggle as the faux Lincoln approaches them. "Ladies, I am Abraham Lincoln. Do you have anything you need freed? Forget my Gettysburg address. Who wants my Lewisburg numbers?"

Another actor approaches from the opposite direction. He wears a white wig and a lab coat. He and the Lincoln actor are rivals and do not like each other. "Forget Lincoln, girls. I am George Washington Carver. Let me show you all the uses for my jumbo black peanut."

"Butt out, Carver. A peanut can't be jumbo."

"Oh, I beg to differ, Mr. President."

"Get out of here or I will un-emancipate your ass."

"I didn't need your mangy ass to emancipate me."

The two shove each other and start swinging and missing. Soon they are wrestling around on the floor. As this happens, a pair of burley types emerge from the manor house and quickly cover the 75 yards or so to the incompetent fighters. The two wear navy blue blazers and khaki pants. One has an eyepatch over his right eye. The other his left. They quickly corral the hack-tors and start hauling them to the manor house when they notice Mark Right. "Hey Mark." "How you doing?"

"Hi guys."

As the four disappear into the manor house, Steve figures it out. "The offensive line?"

"You got it."

A bit farther away Christopher Columbus has wandered near a rather rotund actor dressed as Christopher Columbus. The imposter is not amused. "Hey dude! What goes? I am the Chrissy C around here. I prepared hard for this role. I haven't taken a bath for two weeks! And you just come along. I don't think so." He touches Columbus' clothing. "And your costume. This is the shit dude."

Columbus tries to respond. "Cristobal Colon."

"Don't talk to me like that, freak. This ain't gonna fly. No fancy boy Columbus is gonna take the bread outta my mouth. I'm taking this to the English guy." The actor storms off as Columbus mimics the strange, new language he has just heard. "This is the shit, dude."

Minutes later inside the manor house Garmon Spooneybarger stands in his high-tech monitor-filled control room. He is of diminutive stature with black eyes, a shaved head, and big ears. He wears the previously mentioned red soviet track suit. Having just given his two fighting actors a stern warning he now scans his monitors and notices Mark Right nearby. He picks up a microphone and opens the key.

Outside Mark suddenly hears his name echoing

over the powerful speaker system. "Mark Right, my old friend. Come in and say hello." The door to the manor house opens automatically.

"My God," remarks Steve. "He is Blofeld."

"Let's get this over with," states Mark. Steve parks the cart near the waterfall, and they walk into the manor as the door closes behind them. Soon they are standing in front of Garmon Spooneybarger. A couple more burley types nod in recognition of Mark but this just serves to annoy Garmon. "Hello Garmon."

"Hello Mark. So good to see you."

"I see you shaved off your ratty hair."

"He looks like Blofeld!" Steve whispers to Mark.

"Sir, I do not know this Blofeld, but he would be fortunate indeed to be as handsome as me. Money and power tend to do that to a person. But I guess you would have no knowledge of that."

"Garmon, this is my friend and coworker, Steve Love."

"You should choose better friends, Mr. Love."

"I'm happy with the ones I have."

"I believe you are in the television business, Mark. And that would place you here to help the brilliant J.P. Forte with his calendar girls shoot. They are beautiful women. Nelson and I screened them all personally. One is even a distant relative of mine. She's probably the smartest one. It will be fun watching you two make pathetic passes at them and constantly strike out."

"How is Nelson?" asks Mark.

"He is quite well and as pleased with the mall as I am." And what do you gentlemen think of our creation?"

"It's big," states Steve.

"And expensive," counters Mark. "How did you manage all of this from a two-million-dollar insurance settlement?"

"Connections. Connections. By the way, what do you think of my historical characters? I have, as I once promised you, purchased history."

"Did you build all of this just to spite me about the history thing?"

"Mark, do you really think I would build a 100-million-dollar mall just to spite you?"

"Yes, I do."

"Well, you're right. I did." A creepy smile breaks out on Garmon's face.

"So, taking my prom date, marrying her, and murdering her was not enough?"

"Why do just enough when you can do so much more."

"I guess calling you 'Looneyberger' would not bother you much right now?"

"Not a bit. But you two should be scurrying along. Mr. Forte does not tolerate lateness."

"He's not even here yet."

"Oh, he's here. He is in fact enjoying a repose in the tanning salon." Garmon points to a monitor. "I must say the man's biceps are quite impressive."

"Yuck!" Mark and Steve respond in unison. The door opens and they move toward it.

"Oh, Mark." Garmon raises his hand. "I believe the small café way down the west wing has a special today on French cut green beans. Do enjoy."

As Mark and Steve exit, the Columbus actor squeezes past them. "Another Columbus?" notes Mark. "That one smells terrible," Steve says as he holds his nose. They exit. Mark notices the bottom of a steel security door positioned above the door jamb. The normal door closes, and the actor is grabbed by two members of the security staff.

"Dudes! Let go of me. I want to see the English guy. He's the one who hired me."

"The English guy? Oh, very well." Garmon picks up a bowler hat from a table, places it on his head, and affects an English accent that is more parody than perfect. "Now, old chap, what may I do for you?"

Unbothered by the strange charade, the actor states his gripe. You hired me to play Chrissy C and I saw another one."

"Chrissy C? You mean Christopher Columbus? My dear fellow, you are the only laborer I have engaged to play that role. And you should be out there performing now."

"I saw another Columbus, and he had a fancy suit and a foul mouth."

"That was most likely a Vasco DaGamma."

"Don't mess with me. That Vasco thing is a heart operation. My mother had one."

"Good Lord. Sir, I am going to mess with you and administer a harsh punishment for daring to enter here."

"What punishment?"

"Friend, you are now an employee of the Old Navy store. Take him away."

"No!!!!!!!!!!" The actor is removed to his new post. Garmon takes off the hat.

"It's so hard to get good help."

While walking away from the Manor House Mark has an idea. "Steve, Forte is still tanning, and the girls are not here yet. Let's check this dump out."

"Sounds good, Marcus."

A peek into the east wing reveals a sycamore tree, the golf course, the OK Credit Union, and some construction equipment in the unfinished area. Then Mark spots a prize in the southeast corner of the atrium. "Steve, the jetpack! They spend some time admiring the Bell Rocket Belt which rests inside a velvet rope near the clear elevator shaft. "21 seconds huh?" asks Steve.

"That's all. But the sign says it's fueled up and ready to go, and there's two extra cans of hydrogen peroxide and nitrogen, that's the fuel, sitting there. With a quick refill that's 42 seconds."

"Sounds more like a beauty treatment than rocket fuel," Roadie.

They walk past their cart as they pick up the smell wafting out of Taco Tormento. In the restroom they observe Leonardo sketching a toilet as they splash Garmon's golden urinals. Out of the restroom and now into the west wing, Mark points out a sports collectibles store called, of course, Instant Replay that has reproduction Houston Oilers helmets and Brooklyn Dodgers jerseys that honor a famous lefthander on sale. The pair step to the other side of the wing and take in a display of bipartisan mediocrity in the window of an art store called Brush with Greatness.

"Look Steve, a George W. Bush and a Hunter Biden side-by-side."

"Dude! They both suck!"

"For sure. Bush has a portrait of a sweaty guy that looks like a first-grade finger painting and Biden has something that resembles flowers but not quite. Maybe they're flowers on Mars because that creep has probably been out that far a few times."

Steve reads out the prices. "Fifty dollars for the Bush and 100,000 for the Biden."

"And they're both overpriced."

Trying to erase the horror from their eyes, they

rush next door into The Gift of the Elvi where amusement is quickly gleaned from the contents of the store. Jumpsuits, jackets, Cadillac models, bobble heads of various sized Elvis's. Steve holds up a chocolate bust of Elvis. "Fudge ya. Fudge ya very much."

Mark shows Steve a glass jar that contains a brown and white substance.

"Ugh. What's that?"

"Peanut butter and 'nanner spread, baby."

"Fit for a king-sized stomachache."

Mark is somewhat astounded at the next item he picks up. "Wow. An Elvis toilet seat."

"Fit for a king to fall off of."

"This is kind of on the same level as when Remington released that Hemmingway shotgun." Mark tosses the seat down.

Steve catches something outside the entrance. "Speaking of guns, there's the gun store across the way."

"Then let's leave this building and enter that one."

Inside It's Right to Bear Arms Steve's senses are overwhelmed. "Look at this place! Oh ... oh ... oh ... all my old friends are here! Smith and Wesson, Sig-Sauer, Mauser, Mossberg, Charter Arms, Remington! I'd like to stick my trigger finger there and there and there!" He points to a Sig in a display case. "I could walk into Dick's office with this and say, 'Hey Burley! I'm shooting today after all!'"

"He'd piss himself."

"The only truly meaningful and long-lasting relationships I've had in my life are with guns."

"How about hand grenades?" Mark points to a display case full of them.

"Ooo, ooo, I toss one of those on Dick's desk and say, 'Guess what, Burley? We're going to be roommates in hell.'"

"That's good. Can I use it in my screenplay?"

"Sure thing, roadie."

"At least I've got one line now."

Now a glass display case gains their attention. Inside are the rifles of Davy Crockett and Sergeant Alvin C. York proudly on loan from the state of Tennessee.

"Oh, Steve."

"Oh, Mark."

"Old Betsy is a fine lady," says Mark.

"Sergeant York killed krauts with this very gun," exclaims Steve.

They bow their heads in reverence as they view the next case which holds General Patton's helmet, riding crop, and field glasses. Mark notes that they are on loan from the Patton Museum which is not far away. A store clerk who had been sleeping in the back approaches them. "Gentlemen. Please do not leave fingerprints or drool on the display cases."

"Sir," fires off Steve. "I just want you to know that when I win the lottery, I will be back to buy your entire inventory."

"Oh, what a commission I shall have on that glorious day."

With an annoying clerk now on the scene the pair decide to leave. Noticing that the tanning salon is next door they elect not to risk encountering J.P. Forte and head toward the south wing. Mark is surprised there is no safety railing along the banks of Catgrass Creek, just a one-foot curb where the floor ends and the bank begins. Their first southern stop is at the large window in front of the fitness center watching hot chicks run on treadmills. Unbeknownst to them at this point several of the calendar girls are in this mix.

"I love treadmills," sighs Steve. A squeaking sound near the main entrance catches the duo's attention, and they turn to see Hotwad pushing a large display case on wheels across the atrium.

"There's that idiot with Forte's trophies," warns Mark. "Let's head south." About a half-mile later they are staring at the exterior of Bolsheviky, which features large pictures of Lenin, Stalin, and even one of Tsar Nicholas ll which has a caption that reads 'Check out our Russian Empire section.' Mark points to a tiny picture of Trotsky. "How about that bushy-haired loser."

"I always thought he looked like a sissy."

"He sure couldn't take an ax to the head."

"You'd think that hair would have deflected it."

"Imagine, Steve, we are standing in Larry's backyard on the bank of his little section of Catgrass Creek. The last time we were in this spot we were having a great cookout. Now we are staring at pictures of Russians."

Steve's phone rings. He pulls it from his back pocket, looks at it and answers. "Hello Dick."

"That's Mr. Dick. I just want to make sure you two are at the mall and not at one of the strip joints out that way."

"We're here. Forte is in the tanning booth. Hotwad is pushing trophies around. Mark and I are setting up lights. Although, speaking of strip joints, you should check out the Club Purebred this evening. I hear it's leather pants night."

"Love, you are pushing the limit. I…" Steve lowers the phone and looks at Mark. "You know I've always hated this phone." He tosses it in a trash can as Burley Dick rants on.

Mark gives him a thumbs up. "Mr. Love, I'm proud of you. That's where all cell phones should be. You want to go in this commie place?"

"Fuck Russians. Let's go see Lady Godiva." They trek on. A few seconds later Columbus approaches the trash can and hears Burley's voice drifting out. He pulls the phone out and tries a couple of new phrases. "This is the shit dude."

"Love! Don't talk to me like that!"
"That will be $17.95."
"What the hell?"
"Santa Maria."
"Santa Maria! I knew you were at a strip club." Columbus tosses the phone back in the trash and moves on.

After a quick half mile, the tv-twosome enter the holographic photo store where Steve excitedly approaches Nate. "Can you take my picture with Lady Godiva?"

"No problem. I'm surprised no one has requested her yet. Nate launches his act. The colors swirl. The chandelier glows. Mark takes note of the setup.

"It looks like the Bolshoi. I bet Spooneybarger is behind that."

"Sure is. He's quite a Russia-phyle."
"He's quite a Russia pile."
"Lady Godiva coming up."

Steve is beyond excited. "Coming? I hope so."

Lady Godiva appears inside the arch on a street in Coventry. She sits astride a magnificent white horse holding long reigns made of rich leather. There is no saddle, but she sits on a fine, silk blanket as she is a noble woman. The lady is naked except for a pair of ankle boots with thick soles that seem ideal for kicking an erstwhile Peeping Tom in the gonads. Her blond hair is long but does not, as depicted in legend, cover her breasts, which are quite ample. Her skin is milky white. Her waist is thin and her nether region well-coiffed. The legs are long and smooth. She is beautiful.

Mark is impressed. Steve is frozen. "Steve, she's gorgeous. Steve?" Mark taps him on the shoulder. "Go claim your prize."

"Huh? Oh, yeah. Time to mount." He jumps into the scene and starts to swing a leg up onto the horse.

Nate interjects. "You can't do that, sir. It's a hologram."

Steve pats the horse's butt. "Feels like a real horse's ass. Reminds me of Burley Dick."

"Nice pantomime, sir."

Steve carefully touches Lady G's leg and makes her giggle. "Hey! I heard her laugh!"

"There is no audio in this program. We're still working on that."

Steve gently rubs her left buttock and makes a pronouncement. "She has a crisp apple butt." The Lady busts out (pun intended) into a huge smile.

"Steve, put your arm around her for the picture," reminds Mark.

Steve steps close to the horse and puts his right arm around her waist as she continues her smile. "She smells good too."

"There is no smell," lectures Nate as he pulls the picture from the slot and sleeves it.

"You know, Steve," says Mark, "her name is actually Godifu, which means 'God's gift.'" He hands over a credit card. "And this is a gift from me, buddy."

"Thank you, Marcus." He rubs the noble woman's left hip and elicits another giggle.

Mark takes in the picture. "This is fantastic, Steve."

Hating to leave his position but wanting to see the picture Steve steps down and examines his new treasure. "I love it. I want to order a hundred copies. I'm going to post them all over WDOA."

"They will be ready tomorrow, sir."

The good mood is now wrecked as Hotwad enters. He made the trip south by getting a courtesy ride from a mall worker with a golf cart. After listening to Hotwad talk for the whole one-mile trip the man went to the mall office and quit his job. Hotwad has long, dirty, stringy hair and a thin elongated body looking not unlike an old mop propped outside a cat lady's back door. He wears a black t-shirt with baggy khaki cargo shorts and Wal-Mart brand athletic shoes. His voice grates on one like the squeaky wheel on his trophy cart. "I'm Hotwad. I only have one name like Cher or Madonna."

"Or gonorrhea," states Mark.

"Or syphilis," laughs Steve.

"It's not nice to insult someone you just met."

"We've met like 17 times," glares Mark.

"I'm looking for Steve Love and Mark Right. Mr.

Spooneybarger told Mr. Forte that they were in here."

"We're Steve Love and Mark Right." Mark is not surprised at the idiocy of Hotwad or the fact that Garmon is spying on them.

"Nice to meet you. Mr. Forte is almost done with his tan, and he wants you two to start setting up lights."

"Let's go, Steve. This place just got creepy."

"Watch out for me, Marcus. I'm going to stare at my picture the whole way." Steve blows a kiss to Lady Godiva as they exit. She winks at him, but he doesn't notice.

Hotwad sees the horse but not the naked lady. "Oh, a horse." He looks at Nate. "Why are there horses?"

"What?"

"Why are there horses?"

"How would I know. That's not even a real one."

Not saying anything to a naked lady, Hotwad steps up on the stage and starts playing with the horse's tail as Lady Godiva frowns at him. "Why are there tails?"

"Sir, are you going to buy anything?"

"Why do we buy?" Nate slaps himself on the head, puts up his "BACK IN 15 MINUTES" sign and retreats to the backroom as Hotwad muses on. "If I was a horse, I would not want to have a tail."

CHAPTER 6
Bolsheviks On the Move

1923
The Countryside near Gori, Georgia

The Bolsheviks are sitting around a fire feasting on roast chicken. Stalin sits on a log. The same names and Ivan sit on the ground. Trotsky is standing, refusing to participate in the crude meal. Stalin wipes bits of chicken from his moustache and decides to mock Trotsky. "Bronstein! You should eat. Nasty old kulak woman horded up delicious chickens."

"I am not hungry."

"Perhaps you want western meal. Maybe you want some of the veal that Commodore Vanderbilt eats."

"I told you; he is dead."

"Soon all pigs of capitalism will be dead." He reaches into a pocket for his pipe only to find it missing. "My pipe! My god damnable pipe is missing! Find my pipe you hole-asses!"

Ivan and his charges scramble to their feet then stumble around and run into each other like it is last call at redneck happy hour. "Find it now, you sonless bitches!" Soon they are spread around the area except for Ivan who approaches Stalin and tries to calm him.

"Look on the side of bright, ass of steel. The man at the Gori market for fish say perhaps smoking does not do well for the body that is human."

"What man?"

"The one in charge of the sturgeon. The sturgeon general."

"Fuck the general of sturgeon. He smokes the fish and says others should not. Find my pipe!" Ivan egresses and Stalin starts to undo his pants and heads toward the bushes. "Bronstein! Oak leaves!"

Trotsky mumbles another pathetic "Oy-vey."

Present Day

Mark and Steve are hoofing it north in the south wing. As they approach 'Bolsheviky', Mark notices a small, meek man in a gray suit reeking of anemia and academia as he stares at Stalin's large portrait and smiles. He is carrying a large bag of merchandise that he has purchased from the store. A courtesy cart driver stops by him and offers a ride. The man points south and climbs into the back seat. As the cart whizzes by, Steve looks up from admiring his portrait with Lady Godiva. "There goes a leftist. You can always tell." Suddenly Steve hears a familiar sound and realizes his phone is ringing from the trash can. "Hey, Burley Dick is calling. Hello, Dick."

"Goodbye, Dick," laughs Mark as the pair stroll by.

A few minutes later, attracted by the strange sound, Leonardo Da Vinci approaches the trash can, places his sketch pad on top of it and slowly fishes out the phone. He holds it in his left hand and makes a quick sketch with his right. He looks at it some more and then taps it on the trash can top whereupon Burley Dick's voice emerges. "Love! Love!"

"Love?

"I hear you. You had better start talking or you are finished."

Perplexed by the strange language, the master decides to mimic the sounds of a man suffering from diarrhea, after eating at Taco Tormento, that he just heard in the restroom. Pfffffffffffftttt! Pfffffffffffffttttt! Pfffffffffffftttt!, "That's it, Love! I…C…O…T…I…M…C…I…C! I'm coming out there if my car is charged!" Unfazed, Leonardo places the phone back in the trash and moves on yearning for something better to draw.

After arriving at the holographic photo store and not tipping his driver the meek man approaches Nate. He sits his bag on the counter and gets down to business. "Young man, I was very excited to hear of this enterprise. I teach history over at the University of Lewisburg."

"Well, sir, we can put you anywhere in history that you want to be."

"There is only one place for me. The mighty lion about to assume his throne with a group of lusty young men in tow. Oh, I get so stimulated just thinking about it."

Please, don't get stimulated too close to the computer."

"I want my picture taken with Mr. Josef Stalin in Gori, Georgia in 1923 where he went to recruit an elite personal guard."

"That's a bit specific but I'll see what I can do."

The meek one notices the arch with the Coventry Street inside it. "That looks like the Bolshoi!"

"It's supposed to."

"That street. Looks like England in the 11th century. Maybe Coventry."

"It is but there's supposed to be a naked lady there."

"I have no use for naked ladies."

"I'm not surprised." Nate starts his act.

1923

Stalin emerges from the bushes cinching his pants. "Bronstein, you did not bring me oak leaves. The mighty ass has gone unwiped."

"Why do you defecate all of the time?"

"I do not know this defecate of which you speak."

"Shit! Why do you shit so much?"

"I shit in the face of the west and on the rotting corpse of capitalism. So, I shit often. You should try it, Bronstein."

Ivan and his fellow searchers approach Stalin. Ivan fearfully gives his boss some bad news. "Mighty ass, your wonderful pipe, perhaps it has not been found I fear."

Stalin is outraged and he violently slaps the bolshevism out of Ivan. "Your stench of failure will not be tolerated! Pass it along!" Ivan turns and slaps Sergei #1 who turns and slaps #2. This sequence continues until Sergei #24 is slapped, who, after turning and finding no one to hit, slaps the trunk of a tree fracturing his hand and screaming like Greta Thunberg being forced to ride in a diesel SUV. Or to be more specific for the time period, he screams like the Tsarina Alexandra after Rasputin jumps out of a dark corner to give her a special surprise. His comrades laugh.

"I have a headache," sighs Trotsky.

Stalin thinks for a moment then walks over to the body of the peasant woman. He rummages around her corpse and comes up with a crude corncob pipe. He wipes the tip of it off on his coattail, fills it with tobacco, lights up and takes a draw. "Tastes like kulak." He finishes his distasteful smoke then places his new pipe in his pocket. The mighty ass has decided to load his men into the wagon, then go off to a nearby village, where a woman once spurned him, and have them kill everyone there. Suddenly a wind kicks up blowing leaves, feathers, and Trotsky's hair around. Then an intense orange light starts glowing. The men try to flee but are frozen in place so many of them do the next best thing and wet themselves.

"Oh, dear god," shouts a frightened Ivan before catching a glare from Stalin and correcting himself. "Oh, dear god that is our wonderful Lenin."

Present Day

The lights swirl around the photo stage as Nate completes his act. A couple of feathers drift around the room. "Here come your Bolsheviks." The 27 men appear. The little professor is happier than a looter in a San Francisco Walgreens.

"Oh, dear god that is our wonderful Lenin!"

"Do you smell some kind of feces?" sniffs Nate.

"I smell revolution."

"I smell urine. There should be no smell. I really need to call a service guy."

The enthusiastic customer jumps onto the stage beside Stalin. "Stalin is magnificent! And so many men. Even a dead peasant woman in the background.

Wonderful!"

"I didn't enter that many. But we aim to please."

The man strokes Stalin's moustache as the dictator stares daggers at him in return. "I have never seen a better moustache. And there's Trotsky. That goofy, little dork. I should have brought an ax."

"Your picture is ready, sir."

Not minding the stench, the man mingles with the revolutionaries a bit longer. Then he finally walks over and completes his purchase. "This picture is a work of art. I am going to take the picture of my mother off the wall and put this up. Thank you and have a good day."

The man exits. Nate puts up an "OUT TO LUNCH" sign. "Time for some Taco Tormento." Before exiting he looks back at the Bolsheviks. "See ya later commie-gator." He laughs at his own joke then leaves. A few minutes later, Stalin shakes his head then staggers down from the stage. "What be this place of strangeness?" Trotsky, Ivan, and a few Sergeis follow him down. The rest try to retreat into the image of the countryside but are confined to the area of the stage. "Everyone down now," bellows Stalin. The remaining men assemble, many shaking their legs to alleviate their state of moistness.

"Somehow we have been transported to another location," observes Trotsky as he looks around the room then notices the proscenium arch and chandelier.

"It looks like the Bolshoi."

"Bolshoi!" exclaims Stalin. How we be in Bolshoi? Of course, I have never been, but you would know as you probably went and sat in the Tsar's box with him and sucked on his teat."

"I saw you there many times."

"I ... I only went to fuck ballerinas. Yes. They are very fuckable. I fuck them, and they join the revolution. Yes, that is it." Ivan and the Sergeis, who are regaining their composure, titter and giggle.

Ivan offers up a cheer. "Hail mighty ass! Fucker of Bolshoi ballerinas!" A raucous cheer breaks out.

"Forget ballerinas," yells Trotsky. We must find out what is going on and how we were brought here."

"Magic of black?" asks Stalin.

"No!!!" shout the men.

"Sorcery?"

"No!!!"

Stalin notices an American flag on the wall. "Americans!"

"No!!!"

The Americans are in Moscow! Prepare your weapons!"

Ivan has the Sergei squad ready their rifles as a man enters. "Is this where I can get my picture taken with George Washington?"

"Fuck George Washington," yells Stalin. "Fire!"

"Oh, hell." The man quickly retreats as bullets fly

all around him missing badly like it's an episode of the A-Team.

"Good job, men. One American run; soon they all run."

Trotsky, after some more studying, has an observation. "I do not think this is the Bolshoi. This stage is much bigger. It is a recreation. Perhaps meant to fool us."

"Then where are we to be fooled like this?"

Trotsky stares out the exit into the vastness of the mall. People are buzzing about the gunshots but think it is a performance from actors. "Only one place could be this big. This loud. This expensive. The United States of America."

"How we be in America? How they take us?"

Trotsky points to the computers. "Maybe this machine."

"Kidnap machine. You were in America. Why you not tell us they have kidnap machine? Why do you not tell us they have faculty like this?"

"I did not see a facility like this. There were many tall buildings. Perhaps this was inside one."

Stalin senses the men are frightened. "Men. There is no need to fear yourselves. We are the people's revolution. We cannot be taken for a fool. We will partake of this faculty and devour it. Then we will take all of America! Hail to the revolution! Hail to the mighty ass!"

"Hail to the revolution! Hail to the mighty ass!"

Stalin steps just outside the door where Trotsky is studying a map of the mall that hangs on the wall. "Stalin, this says there is a place called Bolsheviky just ahead of here."

"Then we go there. Men, we march. Bronstein, you bring up the rear. You are good at being in the rear end."

The group marches out into the south wing and immediately cross the foot bridge that puts Catgrass Creek on their right. Stalin is impressed by the smelly tributary and even gives Americans some credit. "Maybe Americans not so dumb. Have ditch inside for shitting in." Some shoppers stare, having no clue who they are. Others react to the smell. Still, others applaud the show. "Hmm," observes Stalin of the applause. "Must be prisoners. We will liberate them before we kill them."

As they march along, the Sergeis jostle and shove many of the shoppers. Ivan knocks Columbus to the ground. A couple of people make a chopping motion at a confused Trotsky's head. Stalin gets a few shout-outs.

"Great moustache, Stalin."

"Stalin! Didn't I see you in a sausage commercial?"

"Hey, Stalin. How's it hanging?" This one gets his attention.

"Hanging? I hang 10 kulaks just last week."

"Kulaks! That's hilarious."

The crewman from the *Titanic* runs by. Iceberg! Iceberg! Dead Ahead!

"Swine pig of capital," barks Stalin.

Mall Headquarters

A security type calls Garmon over and points out the Bolsheviks on one of the monitors.

Garmon is pleased at what he sees. "That's a lot of Russians. Very accurate uniforms. Such a handsome Stalin. Nelson did a good job."

"There are reports of gunshots over there, boss."

"I told him no blanks. He knows how I hate that sound."

South Wing

The band of revolutionaries has arrived at Bolsheviky and Stalin admires three of the four pictures in the window. "Great picture of our beloved Lenin and my wonderful self." He points to Trotsky's small picture. "Good one of you, Bronstein. Just the right size. But American swine put up picture of Nicholas to mock us. Destroy it!" The men smash the glass with their rifle butts, drag the banner out and give it a vigorous stomping. Some shoppers applaud this latest performance.

The store manager runs out to see what the racket is. "What's all the noise ... oh, I see. Bolsheviks. That Mr. Trafalgar sure thinks of everything. You even have the smell. I'll call someone to sweep up the glass." He reenters the store.

"Swine," bellows Stalin. "We kill him first." He points to the banner on the ground. "You men finish your work." The crew descends on the image of Nicholas and tear it into smaller and smaller pieces then toss it into Catgrass Creek. It reminds one of when the real Nicholas and his family were murdered and dismembered by the Bolshevik cutthroats that held them hostage. Trotsky shakes his head as usual. Stalin peeks inside the store at the communist bric-a-brac within. "Americans steal our stuff and put it here. This place will head up our quarters. Ivan! Send out a man to scout how the land is laid ahead." As the ersatz sergeant dispatches one of the less dumb Sergeis on the mission, Steve Love's phone rings from the trash can. Ivan emerges from the startled bunch, slowly peeks into the waste receptacle, carefully extracts the phone and hands it to his leader. It rings again as Stalin shakes it. "Bronstein! What is this?"

"It may be one of those new radio devices for point-to-point communication."

"Love!!!!" Burley Dick's voice shouts from the phone startling the group.

"What is this?" Stalin shouts back.

"Love, I know that's you. That phony Russian accent is not going to fool me. I'm coming your way. There is just a slight delay. I ... H ... A ... P. I hit a pedestrian. Mr. Veal is going to fix it. T ... E ... C ... P... A ... W. These electric cars pack a wallop. When I get there, your ass is grass!"

"If you come here, I will fuck you up your ass that is grass."

"Love!!!" Stalin tosses the phone back to Ivan who tosses it back into the trash.

An enterprising cell phone salesman at a nearby kiosk has witnessed the episode and runs over with the latest model hoping to make a sale. "Mr. ... uh ... Stalin. I see you are unhappy with your phone. Look at this beauty. Can you hear me now?"

Stalin looks the guy over. "Can you hear me now?" He punches him in the face and laughs as the phone guy falls into Catgrass Creek with a splash. "Stupid capitalist. Men! Into the building." The 26 enter and Stalin observes a beautiful crystal, two-headed empirical eagle perched on a not very secure pedestal. "Damnable Tsar eagle." He pushes it off the pedestal, and it shatters into pieces as it hits the highly polished marble floor.

This once again gets the attention of the manager. "That's priceless, you bastard! You goddamned method actors. You're going to pay for that."

"I pay with one bullet." Stalin draws, cocks, and

discharges. If the Taj Ma-Mall reopens after the upcoming troubles, Bolsheviky will need a new manager. He spots another pedestal that is topped by a small glass case that contains his lost pipe. "My pipe! More sorcery is afoot." He smashes the case open with the butt of his pistol, pulls out his pipe then throws in the corncob pipe. As the dictator turns away, Trotsky pulls a small information card out of the case and slips it into his pocket.

The group has fanned out across the store. Several Sergeis find a collection of empirical officers' uniforms and start to swarm it hoping to change clothes and gain a promotion. "Nyet!" yells Stalin. "You already have fine uniform and will not wear the rags of the dog." After the men leave, Stalin spots a pristine, white with a black band and bill, Russian empirical navy admiral's cap on the shelf. He tosses his leather cap away and places the upgrade on his head catching a glimpse of himself in a mirror. "Very handsome."

Trotsky has found a large shelf of Soviet premiere mugs and searches thru them looking for his own likeness. "Stalin … Lenin … Stalin … Stalin … Lenin … man with big eyebrows … Stalin … Lenin … man with red spot on head … Stalin … man with no shirt … Lenin … Stalin … Khrushchev! That goddamned peasant!"

Stalin walks over and picks up a mug with his likeness. "Fine for drinking. Eh, Bronstein?"

"I see you have a new cap."

"I wear this so one of the men cannot. Yes, that is it."

A few minutes later, Stalin is at a large bookshelf looking through a book about the history of the Soviet Union. He has not yet comprehended his movement in time, but he likes what he sees in the book. Trotsky steps over, spots a thin biography about himself and starts to reach for it until Stalin slaps his hand. "There is no time to erupt in reading, Bronstein. We must plan our attack on the Americans." He pats Trotsky on the side of the head and smiles deviously. The two of them simultaneously spot a special display flanked by a large sign that reads "THRONE OF NICHOLAS II." The two despots are drawn to it like they are under a spell. As they try to sit down at the same time, jostling and shoving ensues with Stalin finally pushing Trotsky away and taking the prized seat. "Bronstein, only a mighty ass can sit on the throne of the Romanov pig."

"There is no doubt about that." Trotsky walks off to a quiet corner, retrieves the card about the pipe from his pocket and reads the caption. "This pipe, believed to have belonged to Soviet dictator Josef Stalin, was discovered near Gori, Georgia in the year 2020. Year 2020? Dictator? Something very bizarre is going on."

As Stalin luxuriates on his throne, he is approached by three of his men. One carries a Nagant machine gun. One has the tripod for the gun. Another has an ammo box. "Mighty ass! We find big gun and a box of shooters to place into Americans and make them dead."

"Good work. That is nice gun. It remind me of my first machine gun that I took from the Tsar's men when I was just a boy. Stupid Americans just leave it for us, huh? They still very dumb, even if they have shitable creek. Soon they very dead. When Sergei return with lay of land, we will attack." He rises from his throne and starts undoing his pants headed for the bushes along a very shitable Catgrass Creek.

CHAPTER SEVEN
Meet the Calendar Girls

Mark and Steve have arrived at the atrium, and their eyes are immediately overwhelmed. Scattered about the area are the 12 calendar girls who are preparing for the shoot as they take off athletic shoes and slide out of sweat suits to reveal bikinis and one-pieces while stepping into "work" shoes and putting on their sashes.

Steve's senses are overwhelmed. "I want to put my tongue there and there and there."

"Didn't the judge warn you about that?" Mark teases.

"Fuck the judge."

The duo stand and glower like a couple of mangy redbone hounds staring into the kosher butcher shop. Columbus wanders by quite lost and startled by the almost naked women of this new world. In a clump of bushes on the edge of Catgrass Creek, Leonardo is busy sketching away. But the wonder of the moment is destroyed as Hotwad approaches with instructions.

"Mr. Forte wants you two to know that he has finished his tanning and gone into the gym for some curls. He wants this whole area lit up. You should use lights." He looks around but pretty much ignores the women. "Why is there light?"

"What?" asks Mark.

"Why is there light?"

"So, we can watch you walk away," exclaims Steve. "Bye."

Steve stows away his prized photo in a utility bag on their cart and the two get to work scouting the area for electrical outlets, running extension cords, and setting up their lights. While they are doing this let's meet the calendar girls:

Miss January, Grace Chan, represents Chinese restaurants in Lewisburg and southern Indiana. She has mid-range black hair and wears a one-piece bathing suit from DUE. It has a serpentine dragon, front and back, over a beige base and features multi-colored good luck symbols. She is shod with green Crocs.

Miss February sports a camo bikini from Mossy Oak and long, brown boots from Jones Bootmaker. The oldest of the group at age 34, she has a pleasant round face, a sly smile, straight auburn hair that touches her shoulder blades and adequate boobage. She represents a gun club in southern Indiana called

'Straight Shooters Stop Looters' and is the overall top shooter there.

Miss March, Emma Fleet, stands for the Lewisburg library system and works in the main branch. She is thin with small breasts but sports a prominent butt that she is not fond of. Her light brown hair, streaked with gray, is tied up in a bun. Warby-Parker glasses compliment her face, and she wears a modest one-piece smocked bathing suit in sage green from Geode which makes her look better than she thinks. Black flats from Shoe Carnival finish off the look.

Miss April is Yvonne Lunde, a well-known local gardening advocate and spokesperson for area florists. She blossoms in a floral print bikini from Venus which features a high waisted bottom and a Heavenly halter top, which allows for less tan-lines on the back when working sexily outdoors. A London Fog rain hat sits on top of her strawberry blonde hair that is twisted together into two long braids that each have a pink ribbon tied on the end and boots out of the same label help fend off those showers.

Miss May, Aria Stanzer, is a top jockey at Lewisburg Downs. She is four foot 11 with a strong compact body topped off by a Kari Lake cut of her blondish-brown hair. Her neon pink micro bikini with green polka dots is from the Chynna Dolls collection and echoes jockey silks. The tools of her trade round out this vision, a KEP E-Lite carbon jockey helmet,

Fowler custom made whip and Castillo jockey boots.

Miss June is ironically Lorna Juner. She is nearly 6 feet tall and looks even taller with six-inch green satin stiletto heels by Only Maker and a green French cut bikini from NA-KD that shows off a long stretch of upper thigh. She has long bleach blonde hair but not a good brand of bleach like Clorox more like the Wal Mart house brand. However, if she knew there were ten gallons of hydrogen peroxide over at the rocket belt display, she would likely try to dip into that supply. She represents nepotism as she is a relative of Garmon Spooneybarger.

Miss July, Corporal Jessica Striker, is fit and built as she fronts and is a member of the Army reserve. She presents in a red, white, and blue bikini proudly stitched together by Modlily and wears a pair of her Army boots that she painted to match. Auburn hair is tucked away under her army helmet that is also painted to match the ensemble. The less enlightened members of her outfit refer to her as 'Corporal Cupcake'.

Miss August, Stax Spankster is a talented actress in the Lewisburg adult film industry. She tromps in white boots from SHEIN, stuns with her white bikini bottom from Robin Piccone and draws attention with a blue bandeau top via Tommy Bahama that barely restrains her assets, which are the largest of the group. She has flaming red hair of unnatural origin.

Miss September, Verbota Tubbs, is a hard worker from the bad neighborhood just west of WDOA and is sponsored by the Lewisburg Chamber of Commerce. She is the second shortest of the group and stands out with an unfettered natural hair style, a bright orange, high waisted bikini made by PacSun and Timberline work boots.

Miss October, Channing Gingham, the second tallest of the group, has shoulder length semi-curly black hair and wears a traditional red bikini presented by Nordstrom and yellow Christian Louboutin heels with ankle straps. From a prominent local family of leftists, she is sponsored by several labor unions.

Miss November is Lumina Salazar, fronting her own business inside the mall, Lumina's Salsa Bar, where she does a good trade and makes less people sick than Taco Tormento. She has waist-length black hair, a classic black bikini out of Lascana and black boots from Catherines.

Miss December, one Hilda Gast, is a large girl but still attractive. She has a red plus size one-piece via that woke-tard store that shall remain nameless and red boots thru Kohl's topped off by long, genuine red hair. The local Santa Claus guild is behind her.

As Mark and Steve continue to work, two stereotypes meet when Miss June, who is as dumb as the bargain brand bleach she uses, approaches Miss September, the overachieving hard worker from that sketchy neighborhood, and initiates a conversation. "Like, your orange suit looks so good on your black skin."

Miss September sizes her up. "I would think it does to you girl. You look like a ghost sitting in a box of laundry detergent."

"I wish I could be black."

"Keep working at it, honey. You'll make it someday."

"Thank you. I work out, you know." June flexes her bicep.

"I'm sure it always works out for you."

Miss June pushes her luck. "One of my relatives runs this mall."

"My mother cooks at Taco Tormento."

"That's great. I bet they know each other."

"I bet we should stop talking now."

"Why, thank you. I enjoyed our talk too."

Stereotypes can be funny.

Steve and Mark now have about a dozen lights set up around the area where the south wing meets the atrium, and the creek turns into the waterfall. They have a couple of lights shining down into the sub-atrium. A hotdog vendor parks his cart on the eastern edge of the creek perpendicular to Victoria's Secret and looks toward the duo as he walks away. "Time for lunch at Taco Tormento."

"Why not have a hotdog?" wonders Steve out loud.

"Yuck! I hate those nasty things."

"Must be pork hotdogs because anyone that sells pork is automatically weird," observes Mark. He taps on a large bolder, one of two flanking the end of the creek and butting against the ends of the safety rail that surrounds the top of the sub-atrium and is also utilized down below to keep people away from the waterfall. It is that same double pipe stuff deployed up in the observation deck and is substandard for all three jobs. "This is concrete. Spooney doesn't even have real rocks. And this railing seems pretty flimsy. He removes a flat panel LED light from its case as Steve spots Miss August approaching them.

"We've got company, Marcus, and I think I've seen this one before."

Miss August speaks to Mark. "Take my picture with that."

"This is a light."

Steve grabs the instrument from his friend. "This is a camera. Pose! Baby! Pose!" He puts her thru some paces. Blowing kisses. Putting her thumbs in the sides of her bikini bottom. Bending over and tapping her butt. Running her hands over her hair.

"You're a good cameraman. I'm an actress you know."

"Oh, I know. I'm a fan of your work, Miss Spankster."

"Thank you, but I'm looking for more serious

parts. My agent is trying to get me on one of those reality shows like *60 Minutes* or *ABC World News*."

"Your presence would improve both of those broadcasts."

"My father once told me not to go into show business, but he's an idiot."

"My father once told me to 'Eat leather you little bastard.'" Steve makes a whipping motion.

"My father once saw the handwriting on the wall and made me wash it off," Mark adds.

"You guys are freaks. I like freaks. Send me copies." She pinches Steve on the cheek and walks off.

Miss February struts by and speaks without stopping. "Does this bikini make my IQ look lower?"

Mark is immediately smitten. "Steve, I think I'm in love."

"We'll get you married and divorced yet, roadie."

"I think I've seen her somewhere before." Miss June steps over to address the pair. "Boy that redhead is dumb. I heard her say she likes you guys. It's a shame she can't be on that show *World's Dumbest Blondes*."

Steve attempts to impress. "That show is on our station. We work at Channel 82."

"You two are on television?"

"No, we work in television."

"What show are you on? *World's Biggest Dorks*?"

"We are not on a show; we work at WDOA."

"Then you must be losers." She walks away.

"You know, Steve. *World's Biggest Dorks* gets pretty good ratings, almost as good as *World's Dumbest Blonds.* Man, that Wolf Network."

"We know what show she needs to be on."

Suddenly, Miss February is standing in front of them mocking her coworkers. "My hobbies are cooking, sewing, underwater demolition, and walking around mostly naked in front of horny, desperate men. Wow. They sure rounded up some losers for this gig, right guys?"

"I'm Steve; I will be gripping you today … I mean I will be your grip today."

"Hi, Steve."

"I'm Mark. Will you marry me?"

"That's a direct approach. But I can't marry you right now. I just had lunch."

"There's always supper."

"Never lose that blank, gaping stare. It's quite becoming." She pinches Mark on the cheek and walks away.

"Steve, this never happens to me. This is like some male fantasy written by a lonely, pathetic writer who paid to have his novel published."

"Maybe that's your angle. Male fantasy."

"Better than lonely and pathetic."

A half a mile away, Stalin's hand extends from a clump of bushes on Catgrass Creek. "Oak Leaves! Oak leaves to wipe the mighty ass!" The men go into their usual scramble and there are plenty of leaves around as native plants are still growing along the creek augmented by plastic plants installed by Garmon Spooneybarger. The only large tree in the mall is a sycamore near the manor house. Stalin rejects several offerings, especially the plastic ones until one Sergei hands him a large clump with his gloved hand which is fortunate for this Sergei as Stalin is wiping his mighty behind with oak. Poison oak. Stalin emerges from the clump hitching up his pants when the Sergei he sent on a scouting mission returns. "Mighty Ass! The Americans have many naked women ahead. We must take them to pull our plows."

"Sergeant Ivan! Prepare the men to march." The gang falls into a half-assed formation and sets out. Trotsky brings up the rear again as several shoppers clap and cheer.

At the calendar shoot, the moment of truth is here as J.P. Forte arrives. He is short and scrawny with over-developed biceps that don't match the rest of his body. He has shaggy blond hair and a gray goatee that he thinks looks good. He wears an orange tank top, matching his tanning bed face, to show off the biceps, pre-ripped Jordache jeans and penny loafers with quarters installed in the slots. A canvas camera bag is over his shoulder. He immediately recognizes Steve.

"Steve Love! You old booblicker!"

Mark looks at Steve. "He knows you pretty well."

"Come to soak up some of my genius, you sonuvabitch."

"I hate this jerk." Steve says to Mark.

"Too bad you never got to shoot any sausages, except the one you shoot off with your hand. And there's that guy that works with you."

"I'm Mark."

"I don't care who you are. I just care who I am." He sets his bag on the floor, pulls out a 35mm Nikon and hangs it around his neck. "All right, you skanks. I am J.P. Forte, and I will be shooting this calendar." He retrieves a Sony video camera from the bag and turns it on. "At the same time, I will be shooting a making of video. I can do this because I am a fuckin' genius."

"That's better than a celibate genius," Mark whispers to Steve.

Forte approaches Mark and stares him right in the face. "So, I made me some goddamned vegetable soup last night. It was pretty fuckin' good."

"I think you're nuts."

"Nuts! I like nuts. I should have put me some nuts in that fuckin' soup. Shit!" As he walks away, Mark glances at Steve.

"Who cusses about vegetable soup?"

"Where are our hair and makeup people?" Miss August asks Forte.

"There are no hair or makeup people. My brilliance will make you look good. And with a smaller crew I get paid more goddamned money, which I deserve."

"Are you really that good?" wonders Miss August. "You've never shot any of my movies."

"Anyone who shoots your nasty movies should be shot." Forte recognizes Aria Stanzer. "Hey jockey girl! Every time I bet on one of your fuckin' nags it loses."

"Every time you get out of bed in the morning the world loses."

"I like feisty bitches. I'll whip you into shape."

"I have the whip, jerk."

"Yeah, we're gonna have some fuckin' fun! Now I want you whores to know that JP stands for John Paul which means that I am very pope-like in that I am always right."

"You don't seem that hot," taunts Miss January.

"Hot? Hotwad! Show them some of my awards you long drink of contaminated water."

"Hello, my name is Hotwad." The girls laugh. "You should not laugh at me because I am sensitive."

Miss February has worked her way beside Mark. "Are these guys for real?"

"Sadly, yes. They're called A-listers. All reputation and no talent."

Hotwad displays a trophy from his mobile case.

It is a bronzed doorknob on a wooden base. "Look at that beauty. It's my big bronze knob." Girls laugh, but Forte ignores them. "I won that for my commercials for Laffer Brothers that big home improvement chain."

Miss April speaks up. "My father lost his job when they went out of business."

"Listen, garden girl. My commercials kept them in business longer than they deserved. Show 'em another one Mr. Wad." Hotwad now displays a golden sausage link mounted to a crystal base. Most of the awards in the case are this one. "That's my golden sausage. I've won many of those for my 'Young Bucks' sausage spots."

"It's great sausage," adds Hotwad. "I eat it frozen right out of the package."

"Maybe these guys are performance artists," whispers Miss February to Mark.

"Naw, they're just idiots."

'Show 'em the big one Hot boy. Hotwad flashes a regional Emmy. "That's my regional Emmy. There is nothing better than that."

"How about a national Emmy," yells Mark.

"I will have one of those fuckers soon."

"As soon as one shows up on eBay," Mark whispers to Miss February.

"Time to go to work, you skanks. Love and other guy, turn those lights on. And Steve, I know you brought some skin scorchers shoot one at the fat bitch's ass. Let's clean up that sack of oranges."

"It's ok to be fat now," states Miss December.

"Not in front of my cameras. Fuck! Let's go." With the Sony in his right hand and the Nikon in his left J.P. Forte becomes a foul-mouthed whirlwind. "Move it, sluts. December, over there. March, start marching. February, stop talking to that doofus and get to work. Fuck! April, shower us with some talent, if you can. Stick girl, you've got no tits. Why are you here? Oh, I see, keep your back to the camera. January, drag your dragon ass over there. September, you've got work shoes, work! October! Move those over-priced Christian Louboutin's! You sluts are all ugly. I've seen prettier rats. Fuck-a-doodle-dick!"

"Fuck-a-doodle-dick?" Mark says to Steve. "Now he's making them up."

"Assholefuckinmoron," answers Steve.

Forte laughs. "That's a good one, Love. Now adjust some fuckin' lights. July! Stand at attention!"

Steve looks at Mark. "She makes me stand at attention."

"Ramrod straight," adds Mark.

Forte continues his process. "Skankwhores, if we all work together, we can make me look damned good. May! Ride somebody. Jump on the fat one's back."

"I will not."

"Read your contract—you will. June! You should

be November cause your ass and tits are both turkeys. Long hair, walk across the creek like you're sneaking into the country."

"I'm a fifth-generation American."

"I don't care. July, get down there and have sex with that waterfall. Jockey, ride that boulder. Shake your asses. I swear I have a better ass than any of you bitches."

"Like, you are the biggest ass," tosses Miss June.

"Like, shut up, bitch. July, pretend that something is screwing you. Hotwad, I see you sleeping. Polish my bronze knob. Dragon boobs! Give me some of that Chinese jibber jabber."

"I can't speak Chinese."

"You are all pathetic! Piss on a duck!"

"You shouldn't piss on ducks," cries June.

It's like you bitches don't want me to win another award."

"We want you to drop dead," yells Miss September.

"That's the attitude I need. Give me more, ghetto girl. May! Start whipping these bitches!"

Miss February has an idea for Mark. "Other guy, you want to sneak down there by that waterfall and make out?"

Mark is stunned at the proposal. "Brrr ... errr ... braaaa..."

"I'll take that as a yes." She takes his hand and leads him down the short stairway to a dark corner on the far left of the sub-atrium. Mark usually stays away from the left side of anything but will make an exception in this case. Steve notices and smiles.

Over in the mall HQ Garmon has been watching the monitors with his security staff. "That Forte is really working them. I've heard he was a genius, and I can tell. It takes one to know one. Where did Right and that girl go?"

"Down by the waterfall, boss. There's no camera there."

"Then we need to put one there. That creep's probably doing perverted things to her, and we should be watching. We sure saved enough money on those cheap Chinese safety rails to buy more cameras."

"Mr. Spooneybarger, those Russians are about to enter the atrium."

"Must be time for another show."

"They've got a machine gun, boss."

"That's the one from the Bolsheviky store. I told the manager to lock up the bullets. I don't know why they sent bullets with it anyway."

"What if he didn't lock them up?"

"Then he would be fired. Now, let's just sit back and watch this fine theatrical. It should be fun."

CHAPTER 8
Hitting the Fan

As Nate, the holographic photo clerk, returns to his post, he finds an impatient woman and her nine-year-old son waiting for him.

"It's about time someone showed up. We've been waiting. I don't have all day." The woman barks.

Nate steps behind his console and points to the "OUT TO LUNCH" sign as he takes it down. "Just stepped out for some lunch. That Taco Tormento is intense."

"I don't want to hear about your nasty lunch, loser. Get your ass to work; my son wants to see some dinosaurs now."

'Yeah," adds the rancid kid. "See some dinos now, you pathetic freak."

"Young man, it's not nice to talk to people like that. My name's Nate."

"We don't care what your name is, jerk. Get to work, or I'll have your low-paid ass. And no worthless plant eaters, he wants T-Rexes."

"Yeah, T-Rexes, you low-paid ass."

"Coming right up." Hoping to end the encounter as soon as possible, Nate skips most of his act and quickly punches a couple of buttons. The stage is soon crammed with the legs of Tyrannosaurus Rexes.

"Dinos! Dinos! Mine!" shouts the kid as he jumps up on the stage and starts kicking the legs. "Growl, you bastards! Growl!" Growls are elicited, which Nate dismisses as the kid making the noise.

"Those are just legs," shouts the woman. "Where's the rest of them? I'm not paying for just legs."

"It's a big image, ma'am. See, there's a head now." A T-Rex lowers its head to size up the kid just as a small planteater called an Albertadormeus Syntarsus peeks out from between the legs. The kid is not impressed.

"What a shitty Dino." He punches the Albertadormeus in the head, and it decides to try meat by biting off his hand. "Mother fuck!"

"Don't you use that word."

The T-Rex has made his lunch choice, and the kid becomes a brat McNugget with one mighty chomp.

"Oh my God!" screams the woman as she passes out on the floor.

"Fuck!" shouts Nate, who sizes up the situation, and then puts up his "OUT TO LUNCH" sign, runs out the exit, sharply turns left and out the service door.

The terrible lizard jumps off the stage and quickly reunites the woman with her son. Then, an attractive scent is picked up, and he smashes through the large wall between the stage and the computer area to enter the food warehouse. He is followed by five more of his kind and the small Albertodormeus, who is usually a T-Rex food source, but he should be safe while the big boys are otherwise occupied.

And they should be situated here for a while. As this all happens, Christopher Columbus walks in and catches a glimpse. "This is the shit, dude!"

In the mall office, a security guy has caught the action on a monitor. "Hey, Boss, there are dinosaurs in that photo place."

"Of course there are. They're holograms you idiot."

"Uh, ok boss. Oh, it looks like those Russians are about to do something."

Stalin has sized up the photo shoot. The girls are now bunched up on the western side of the atrium. He approaches, unperturbed by the abundance of female flesh. He has told Ivan and 22 of the Sergeis to fan out around the area. The other two Sergeis are setting up the Nagant atop the fake boulder on the eastern bank of the creek. The girls don't notice, as they are too busy being harangued by J.P. Forte. Steve is a bit alarmed but figures they are actors. He tries to show Hotwad what is going on but is waved off by the wadster who is busy playing Candy

Crush on his phone. A smattering of shoppers look on watching the show. Trotsky takes a position to Stalin's left, unsure about the whole operation. Stalin pulls and cocks his pistol and fires one shot into the air. A man falls from the observation deck screaming and meeting his demise. A few shoppers applaud the stunt performance. Others creep toward the exit. Steve is outraged.

"Dude! You just killed somebody. Really? You goddamned method actor!"

Forte is more outraged. "Who the fuck is interrupting my genius with a fuckin' cap gun?!"

"Shut up your fuck face! Fucklicker!" bellows Stalin.

"Whoa! That's good shit." Forte produces a small notebook and pencil from his back pocket and makes a note.

Miss March is surprised to see figures from the Russian history section, "Stalin and Trotsky?"

"I see we are proceeded by our own refutiation. I am very much Josef Stalin, Chairman of the Central Committee and this is indeed Commissar Trotsky (Stalin laughs.) as you infidels might know him."

"Nice hair, freak," laughs Miss May at Trotsky.

"I declare this faculty as the property of the people's revolution, and everyone here is now a prisoner of the Union of Soviet Socialist Republics. We will make you naked women pull our plows."

"Have you ever heard of a tractor, dumbass?" asks Miss April.

Stalin notices Miss July. "America girl. You will pull the plow first."

"I will pull off your phony moustache and shove it up your ass."

Miss October has approached Stalin. "You are very handsome."

"This, of course, I know. Maybe you pull plow last."

"I will pull anything you want me to. I had your picture on my bedroom wall in high school."

Ivan is overcome by his hormones. "I want to have sex with big cow!"

Miss December takes offense. "Hey, jerk! It's ok to be fat now."

"I think he means a real cow," adds Steve.

"That's pretty kinky, even for my neighborhood," says Miss September.

Miss August is curious. "Did my agent send you guys? You smell just like him."

Steve is starting to sort things out. "These guys are either awful good actors or..." he thinks out loud. "Lady Godiva's ass felt very real."

Miss August stomps over to Steve and places his right hand on her ass. "Was it better than this?"

"You're here now, so yours is better."

"Good answer." She kisses him on the cheek.

"Stalin, Trotsky," Steve yells. "What year is it?"

Trotsky fields the question. "In Russia, we have changed the calendar so no one really knows what year it is, but you in the West would call it 1923."

"Yeah, dude, you're a bit off."

Over in the sub-atrium, Mark and Miss February have broken off their activities and are listening to the scenario playing out in the atrium. "What the hell is going on up there," wonders Mark. "Stalin and Trotsky? And there's a dead guy? He hears some racket about ten feet above his head and just to the right of his position. He looks up to see the barrel of the Nagant protruding over the concrete boulder. "A machine gun?"

"Terrorists?" asks February.

"Maybe terrorists from time. Steve said Lady Godiva felt real."

"Lady Godiva?"

"Steve had his picture taken with her at the hologram place."

"How about you?"

"I'm waiting to have my picture taken with you, of course."

"Good answer." She kisses him on the cheek.

Upstairs Hotwad is still oblivious to everything until Trotsky approaches the mobile case and reaches for a trophy. "You should not touch Mr. Forte's bronze knob."

"I beg your pardon."

"Why are you the guy in my history book with an ax in his head?"

"Ax? What ax?"

Not wanting Trotsky to ask more questions, Stalin gestures toward the two Sergeis at the Nagant then gives his orders. "Enough! Take the cows!"

The machine gunners start spraying the area. The other men are mesmerized and hesitate in starting their attack. Shoppers run toward the two-dozen doors, and many make it, yet others are cut down. A man and his nagging wife are walking toward the exit. He carries a cartoon-like load of packages. She provides what she considers advice. "Careful. Don't drop that crystal. It cost most of your paycheck. Watch it. Watch it. Do you know how to walk? Left … right. Come on."

Bullets rip through the man, and he drops like a diving mule at a county fair from back in the day before it was considered cruelty to employ mules in a perk-filled job where they were well treated. "What are you doing? Get up! Ron? I told your dumb ass you couldn't carry all of that. Ron? Ron?" Ron is not getting up. A few more bullets, and she follows.

In the mall office, one of Garmon's security people runs in from the atrium. "Boss, the Russians are shooting people!"

"Yes, I know. It's quite a spectacle."

"No, boss, they got real bullets. People are dead."

"Dead! What the bloody hell! The lawsuits are going to cost me a fortune. You guys get out there and stop this."

"We don't have guns. You wouldn't let us carry guns."

"Then go to the gun store and get some."

"Those guys shooting are between us and the gun store."

"Then use a tunnel."

None of the tunnels go over there."

"Then fuck!" He picks up a microphone and speaks in a calm voice. "Attention mall patrons. There is a very minor security issue happening right now. Please evacuate the mall in an orderly fashion."

At the cinema, a few minutes later, the evacuation is large and intense. Two men approaching from the parking lot see the egress, and one looks at the other. "Tom Cruise must be doing a love scene."

In the sub-atrium Mark is searching for a plan. "We've got to stop that machine gun. And when I woke up this morning, I never thought I would be saying that." He notices an old-style Fresnel light he set up earlier blazing away at the waterfall with its yellowish glow. "That thing is red hot. If I could toss it up there." He reaches for his back pocket. "I left my gloves upstairs."

Miss February strips off her bikini top and tosses it to him. "Use that."

"Baa … ber … ba … ber … ber…"

"You can look at those later. We've got work to do." She turns the light off, unplugs it and loosens the clamp. Mark recovers enough to grasp a B cup in each hand, lift the light off the stand and heave it above his head and to the right. "Let there be light."

Upstairs a Sergei sees the light flying toward him and instinctively grabs it. "Der' mo! (shit) he screams and tosses it to his partner.

"Chort voz' mi!" (Damn it to hell), screams the other as they toss it back and forth a couple of times before slinging it into the creek where it sizzles away.

Mark runs out of the sub-atrium carrying the light stand. Miss February follows, strapping on her warm top and adjusting her sash. One machine gun Sergei is jumping around shaking his hands; Mark smashes him in the face with the light stand and puts him down. The other gunner is on his knees cooling his hands in the stream. Miss February jumps on his back, forces his head underwater and gurgles him into unconsciousness.

An irked Stalin fires a shot in the air, urging his distracted men on. "Men! Take these bitches now!" Twenty-two Sergeis and Ivan turn their attention to the 11 girls in the immediate area. Since these men were pulled from the hinterlands and not trained very well, they are rather poor fighters in hand-to-hand combat, hence their chicken coop adventure.

As the battle escalates, Trotsky jumps behind a potted plant to secure the area there. Hotwad plays Candy Crush, and J.P. Forte makes a decision. "I'm getting my hairy white ass the fuck outta here." He stuffs his cameras in his bag and runs into the west wing.

Forte's egress does get Hotwad's attention. "Mr. Forte! Your awards!" He pushes his cart in the same direction.

In the mall office, Garmon is concerned about the battle and makes his own decision. "Total mall lockdown! Now!" One of the security guys pushes a prominent red button and steel plates slam down over every entry/exit and window in the mall, Manor House included, sealing it off from the outside world. Shoppers and actors still trapped inside scramble to find hiding places.

Mark and Miss February are now behind the machine gun but don't have a shot as the combat before them is hand-to-hand. The women are fighting viciously. August screams out, "Come on, creeps! I know Tie Kwan Dye!" January, who does know Tai Kwan Do, chops an attacker down. "I'll drop you bitches like shrimp into a deep fryer." March stomps on a foot then kicks a shin. "We have lots of self-defense classes at the library, bozo." April unleashes a nasty punch to the gut. "Lifting fertilizer bags makes you strong." Then she tosses her rain hat into her attacker's face and snaps him in the eye with the end of a braid. May is wielding her whip, effectively bashing Sergeis, and she hits one on the hand—the guy with the broken hand—and he gains a second fracture, which makes her move extra effective. "I'll whip you bastards into the dust bin of history." June hides behind a trash can, planning on taking credit if any successes occur.

July, who is a trained fighter, knocks several Sergeis around and has now squared off against Ivan. He punches her in the face, which she shakes off and returns a couple of gut shots. He punches her again, and she ducks a couple more shots. Suddenly, she removes her top and waves it in the air. As Ivan stares at her boobs, she kicks him in the nuts and tit slaps him to the ground strapping her top back on all-in-one stimulating motion.

Steve is standing at attention nearby and saluting. "I love this country."

August doesn't really know any martial arts but is implementing an effective bitch slap she developed from years of fending off the advances of film producers. "It's time for my closeup, bastards."

September jerks the rifle off an attacker's shoulder and smashes the stock over his head breaking it off. She flips the gun in the air then hits him with the barrel, fracturing it and the guy's skull. "You creeps wouldn't last five minutes on my street."

November is efficiently utilizing her shiny black boots cracking shins and kneecaps. "If you actors, or whatever you are, need a break after getting the shit beat out of you, I have several specials today at my salsa bar."

December is quite good at running into Sergeis and knocking them down while shouting, "It's ok to be fat now."

Trotsky does not like what he is seeing and briefly jumps out from behind the sanctuary of his potted plant. "We are losing this fight to mostly naked women. This is not the people's revolution."

Frustrated, Stalin yells an order. "Sergeant Ivan! Take back the damnable machine gun! Now!"

Ivan motions three of his least damaged men toward the gun. Two run directly toward it. The other cuts wide to the right.

Steve runs up to Stalin and punches him in the face putting the mighty ass on his ass. October shoves him out of the way. "Don't pick on him, you creep."

"Whose side are you on, bitch?"

"I'm for the people's revolution!"

"Good, Lord." Steve shakes his head then runs toward the east side of the atrium yelling out to Mark. "I'm coming your way, roadie!"

October helps Stalin up while slipping his pistol out of its holster.

The two running Sergeis have reached the west

bank of the creek. Mark fires a machine gun blast at their feet, feeling a sensation like never before. "Whoa! Whoa! Wow!" He hears a crashing noise behind him and sees the hotdog cart, which had moved toward the creek fueled by earlier vibrations from the gun, crashing into the stream. "That's some fast food." The two menaces continue to approach, and Mark faces a decision. "I think I'm going to have to kill them."

"Do your duty soldier," urges February.

Mark unleashes another blast and shoots the pair into a bloody pile as Steve approaches from the east. "Mark, you killed those two really good."

"I … I … uh…"

"It was them or you, brother."

The third advancer, who is the grenade-bearing Sergei, pops up from a clump of bushes on the far side of the creek and pulls the hard stick from his pants. February cuts out toward the threat. "I've got him."

"No! Wait!" yells Mark.

February tackles the attacker forcing the grenade to make a truncated flight from his hand landing on the hotdog cart. She punches him in the face then pulls him over her as a shield. The grenade detonates setting off the propane tanks in the cart and creating a fireball as huge as if Brian Dennehy had eaten at Taco Tormento. The following kinetic wave lifts Mark and Steve into the air leaving Mark just enough time for a quick witticism. "You'll believe a man can fly." The endangered duo crashes through the display window of Victoria's Secret; presumably dead.

Shoving the shrapnel-filled remains of the Sergei off her, February screams, "No!"

October, with Stalin's pistol in her hand, pulls June from behind the safety of her trash can and shoves the barrel into her right ear. "You sluts give up, or I'll waste this whore."

"Like, no one has ever paid me for sex, bitch," protests Miss June.

May continues to slash at Sergeis with her whip. "She's not worth it. Keep fighting, girls."

"At least if her brains get blown out it won't make much of a mess," assures September.

"Thank you, friend," misconstrues June.

Stalin walks up to October and pulls the hammer back on the pistol. "Now mind of bitch ready to be blown."

"Come on, girls," cries June. "You can't have a calendar without June."

"In Russia, we have calendar without a lot of months," says Stalin.

July, with her military training assesses the situation. "We can't let them kill her."

"Yes, we can," shouts September.

"We'll surrender err … I hate that word, briefly, then escape and regroup. These clowns can't hold us."

Stalin takes his pistol, pats October on the butt and tells Ivan to have his battered crew herd the woman into a group.

May reluctantly hands her whip to a Bolshevik. "Take care of this. I'll need it later to bash your head in."

July directs some ire at October. "What is this? You traitor. You take up with a bunch of fake commies. They're out of control method actors, dumbass."

"Oh, they're real. I know it."

"How can they be real?"

February, who has been forced into the group by the previously gurgled now recovered Sergei, agrees with the bikinied peril. "Something's going on with time in the mall. I think they ... are ... real."

The girls are stunned but December senses an opportunity. "Time travel? Can I go back about 30 pounds?"

October is elated. "I knew it. They have come through time just for me." She pulls down her left cup halfway revealing a hammer and sickle tattoo on top of her breast.

"Really, bitch!" screams July.

"It's so small," observes January.

"And the tattoo is small, too," adds April.

"Shut up, jealous sluts. I am going to be queen of the Soviet Union."

"I don't think they're into monarchs," warns March.

"Da, we take care of you," assures Stalin.

October touches Stalin's left arm. "I can take care of you. I know this arm was injured when you were a handsome young lad. Some creep in a carriage ran over it. How sad.

"Yeah," yells May. "It was sad he didn't run over your head."

"Now, March!" yells Stalin.

"Yes," March responds.

"He means we march," says February.

"That's hard in these boots," observes August. "I'm going to fire my agent for this shitty gig."

"And as we march, we plot to avenge Mark and Steve," vows February.

Trotsky mutters to himself. "The revolution is doomed."

October touches Trotsky on the shoulder. "Only you are doomed, Bronstein." Stalin smiles at her. The women, flanked by the Sergeis, many hampered by their injuries inflicted by the calendar girls, are forced toward Bolsheviky, which is half a mile away. Stalin, October and Ivan lead the way with Trotsky toward the rear, trailed only by "light stand" Sergei, who stumbles along with his smashed face and seared hands. After a moment Stalin sends two of his least damaged men back to retrieve the machine gun.

The Sergeis, now number 21 with the two shot down by Mark and the one who collected his own shrapnel subtracted.

Unseen in the bushes, Leonardo DaVinci sketches away.

CHAPTER 9
A Half-Priced Thong and a Vodka Filled Toilet

It has been a couple of hours since the biggest mall fight in history, outside of Black Friday. Inside Victoria's Secret, amid broken glass, fractured mannequins and women's undergarments, Mark and Steve are beginning to come around.

Mark leads off the recovery. "Oh ... God. What happened? I feel like Melissa McCarthy is sitting on my head."

"We were fighting Stalin and Trotsky and a bunch of Russians. Then a grenade went off, and we got blown through the window of Victoria's Secret."

"Steve, I bet you're the only person on earth to utter that sentence today.

"I'm surprised we're not dead."

Mark holds up a bra. "We landed on a padded bra display."

"I love this country."

Mark glances around at the scattered undergarments. "Looks like your bedroom floor on Sunday morning."

Steve's right hand rests on the crotch of a mannequin that lies parallel to him. He feels around and thinks it is part of himself. "Nooooooo! Little Steve! Little Steve is gone! He was in the prime of life."

"That's not you."

Steve catches on and feels his own crotch. "Thank God for small favors." He notices something on Mark's head. "Dude. Nice hat."

Mark pulls a black thong off his head and studies it. "Hey. Half price."

"You should buy that for your new girlfriend."

They stagger to their feet and look out the window. "Where are the girls?" Mark asks.

Taken by Stalin and the commies?"

"So, I finally meet a girl and lose her to Stalin?"

"What the hell is going on here, Marcus?"

"Some serious Art Bell type stuff."

"Art Bell. He was good."

"Yeah, I miss him. George Noory is on now, but it's not the same.

Garmon Spooneybarger and a couple of his security people enter. Garmon looks at Mark with disdain. "Right. What the fuck? Actors are shooting people. My beautiful atrium is trashed. People are dead. I'm going to have to send Nelson out to tell the fucking media that everything is fine, and I've got the feeling that you know what the hades is going on."

"Those are not actors. Your holographic photo booth is some kind of time machine. Stalin and Trotsky are here."

The crewman from the *Titanic* runs by. "Iceberg! Iceberg! Dead ahead!"

"I suppose that guy is really from the *Titanic*?"

"Probably. None of the actors you hired would be that dedicated."

"Nelson hired the actors."

"You are Nelson."

"Stalin is here? I've always admired him."

"Says the man wearing the soviet tracksuit," Mark mocks.

"Time travel? That could be quite lucrative. I could offer tours through time. I could charge a fortune for something like that. And perhaps I could go back and obtain some Soviet construction contracts to build shoddy apartments that would collapse during a steady breeze. Then I could build them again and get paid again. Dad would be proud of me."

"This is not a good thing. You've got dead people. And some people lying out there might still be alive. Do you have a medical staff?" Mark is incredulous.

"There's a nurse somewhere, but she's probably drunk."

"Get your staff together. Look for people to help. Cover up the bodies. Show some respect and dignity. Steve and I are going to get some guns and rescue the girls."

"Yeah, boss. We need some guns too."

"No one is getting any guns."

Steve stares him down. "What the hell, dude?"

"When the mall is in lockdown, the gun store is also sealed off by a thick security door. And I'm not going to open it lest guns fall into the wrong hands."

"The wrong hands already have guns," yells Steve. "So, we'll just break into the damned place."

"You could try to pick the mechanical lock on the door, but it's impenetrable.

Mark is becoming irritated. "Is there a real sporting goods store here besides the classic place? We could get some bats and golf clubs, at least."

"I am proud to say that Dick's is coming soon to the east wing."

"Dude!" shouts Steve. "We're getting dicked right now."

"Listen, Looneyburger, we need weapons," urges Mark.

"Then scrounge about the area. Maybe you can turn up a sharp stick or two."

"Come on, Steve. Let's go." The two limp off toward the atrium.

Outside the mall, first responders are arriving

from every direction. This includes fire and police from several counties away. There are rumors that the Kentucky National Guard is on the way. The media hordes have been herded into an area near the employee entrance halfway down the southern wing. This spot includes a bank of bright blue portable toilets for employee use, as Garmon won't let his underlings use the ritzy indoor restrooms. So, it is the perfect area for the media to gather.

In the nearby bushes, a hatch opens and Nelson Trafalgar climbs out. He is clad in his English outfit with waistcoat, gray trousers and a top hat. Quick recognition follows and the locusts descend on him.

"It's Nelson Trafalgar. What's going on with your mall, Mr. Trafalgar?"

"Is it true that shots have been fired inside the mall?"

"Are actors with guns shooting people?"

The WDOA reporter, with his wavy hair, digs deeper. "Mr. Trafalgar, are you gay?"

"Pip, pip, dear friends. There is nothing to be alarmed about. A minor disruption occurred inside the mall, and Mr. Spooneybarger initiated security measures that are designed to protect the general public. The mall security staff is on top of it as we speak." Over at the hatch, several members of that security staff have climbed out and are literally sneaking away behind Nelson's back. "The security detail here is made up of crackerjack troops. They were trained by the King's Beefeaters."

"So, you admit to eating an unhealthy amount of beef?"

"I admit nothing except the tip-top condition of my staff who would willingly take a bullet for me."

"Your staff shot at you?"

"Did they shoot at you because you are gay?"

"This interview has ended. Tally ho and all."

Back inside, Steve has looked around and found the remains of the gun that September bashed a Sergei with. He also found Miss April's rain hat with blood on it, and prayed that it was enemy blood. As he walks toward the west wing, Mark comes out of The Gift of the Elvi carrying a couple of objects. "Ah, you found a gun."

"It's pretty beat up, but it's loaded, and I might get a shot or two out of it. What have you got?"

"Letter openers. See the king's head on top. From the early period. They're really sharp though." He hands one to Steve. They stuff them into their back pockets then hear a creaky sound approaching. Steve points the gun in the direction of the sound as J.P. Forte approaches, followed by Hotwad and his squeaky cart.

"Don't shoot, Steve. Fuckaroni!"

"Why have I wet myself," wonders Hotwad.

"I should have fired first and asked questions later," rues Steve.

"What in the holy fuck is going on in this bitched up place?"

"Let's see," explains Mark. "There is a time warp in the mall. Stalin and Trotsky are here. They took the calendar girls. Oh, and you two ran off."

"Time warp! That's some messed up shit." He and Hotwad spot the bodies strewn around the atrium. "Country fried cock!"

"Why are those dead people, dead?"

"You two could be next," warns Mark. "So, stay the fuck out of the way. Steve and I have a job to do."

"Where do you think the girls are, roadie?"

"Those commie creeps must be drawn to that Russian store. I bet we find the girls there."

"Let's roll. Stalin's got a fight coming, and he's got it today."

"We'll swing by the golf course and look for a club. I think a driver would suit Stalin's head."

They trek off toward the east wing as Forte watches and yearns. "Time warp. Hmm, I wish I had me some of that goddamned vegetable soup."

"Why is there soup?"

"Hotwad. Shut the fuck up."

At the junction of the atrium and the east wing, Mark steps onto the putting green that rests under the sycamore tree. He quickly finds a putter, looks in the cup and pulls out a ball. He steps back some, sets the ball down and lines up his putt. Even with Bolsheviks to kill, there is always time to practice a ten-footer. Steve hears a noise in the tree, sees a gun barrel pointed at Mark and fires off a shot. A Sergei falls from the tree and lands on the green on his side followed by his rifle. The Sergei can only utter one final thought. "May I please drive your automobile, Mr. Ford."

"Whoa! Thanks, Steve."

"No problem, buddy. Besides, I think the really heavy Bolsheviks won't be coming down for quite a while yet."

Mark studies the position of the Sergei's body that now lies between his ball and the cup. "I think you lined up my putt for me." He taps the ball. It contacts the Sergei at his hand, travels along his outstretched arm, goes past the shoulder, down the back, around his butt and then straight down the leg, finally rolling off his heel and into the cup. Mark runs around waving his putter like Chi Chi Rodriguez. "Mark Right wins the Bolshevik classic!" The two security guys that Mark met when he first entered the mall approach him and Steve.

"Mark Right. Spooneybarger is crazy."

"Yeah, the police keep calling and asking him to open the doors, but he won't do it. He says he's going to take care of it himself. He's locked us out of the controls, so we can't do it either."

"All the staff has quit and bugged out except for us."

"Well guys, like you said, he is crazy. Stick around

here and do what you can. Maybe look for blankets to cover up the dead. And if it comes to it, take the bastard out." He hands over the putter and picks up the Sergei's rifle. "Steve and I have calendar girls to save."

"Good luck, Mark Right."

"Godspeed."

About 20 minutes later, Mark and Steve approach Bolsheviky from the east and opposite side of the creek and see that the commies have laid out a compound by raiding the Crowe's Furniture store that sits across from Bolsheviky and using the major appliances to build walls. On the Bolsheviky side of the creek, a wall of washers, dryers, refrigerators and dishwashers extends from each side of the store to the bank of the creek. Right in front of the store, Stalin has set up his throne. In front of that is a toilet filled with vodka looted from the mall's liquor stores. The men dip out of it with Stalin mugs.

On the other side of the creek, where Steve and Mark are, Crowe's Furniture consists of two parts: the store itself and a large open area on its southside that features artificial grass and patio furniture. This is the place the Bolsheviks have walled off with appliances from wall to creek to imprison the girls. Beside the creek "skull fracture" Sergei sits on a dishwasher. Hoping to prevent more damage he wear's Aria Stanzer's helmet on his small head. In front of him is another dishwasher with the Nagant machine gun on top of it pointed at the prisoners. Near the gun, next to the creek bank, two Sergeis are feeding a bonfire. It seems the prisoners asked for their personal items, including duffel bags, sweats and athletic shoes, to be brought to them; these two retrieved the items and are burning them to mock the women while emitting an occasional "Moo" in their direction. Of course, they don't know what the cell phones are, but they enjoy watching them melt.

Ten of the girls are in the makeshift prison with 'light stand' Sergei standing guard nearby. All other Sergeis are scattered throughout the mall scavenging the spoils of capitalism. Aria Stanzer sits on a dishwasher that is part of the northern wall with her back toward Mark and Steve. She is gagged and wrapped in eight strands of rope as she was too much to handle and listen to. Stalin, Trotsky, and Ivan are nowhere to be seen. Just north of the makeshift wall on the eastern promenade is parked a mall courtesy cart. The commies have messed with it and are thinking about harnessing some of the women to it to pull it around and haul back more vodka.

As the guys move closer, Mark sees October on the far side of the creek handing leaves to a hand protruding from the bushes. A couple of minutes later, Stalin steps out, fastening his pants. "Very good oak leaves, da." He scratches his ass once, then takes October by the hand. "Let us go and make mockery of our prisoners." Together they start to walk across the shallow creek.

Mark and Steve duck into Crowe's, where Mark looks around and comments, "How about that great wall of appliances? That's the only way Crowe's can move their cheap shit. Give us a 'caw,' and we'll send a Russian over with a Mexican refrigerator."

"They've cleaned everything out of here except the beds," Steve observes.

"I guess when you're used to sleeping on piles of cow shit, you don't really know what beds are for. We should check something though." Mark quickly looks under all the beds to make sure no commies are hiding there. "I think we're ok."

Outside, Stalin and October are reviewing the prisoners.

Miss July yells out. "Stalin, give us five minutes with that traitor bitch." October gives her the finger, and then pats Stalin on the ass which causes him to scratch again.

"My men capture very lively group of captivators."

June looks at Stalin. "My friend, September, says you are from history. Like you're that Napoleon guy."

"Fuck Napoleon," roars the mighty ass. "Small-cocked little prick."

"That's redundant," points out March.

"Bitch," September scolds June. "I told you he was Stalin."

"Like what's he stalling about?" stammers June.

"He's Josef Stalin from Russia," you high-thighed twit.

"Like, how do you know anything about history anyway?"

"Like, I stayed awake in class."

"Like, Stalin, I can't wait to kill you and your creepy men," adds February.

"You naked women in position to kill no one, just pull plows. October, we go, I read you favorite passages from history book I find. Sergei, Sergei, Sergei come along and drink vodka. Sergei, stay behind gun."

"Bye, bitches," laughs October as she takes Stalin's hand and they stroll off to a chorus of hisses and catcalls. The three Sergeis head to the toilet. Stalin sits on the throne as October jumps on his lap.

Steve glances at Mark. "What the hell. Are they all named Sergei?"

"Soon, they will all be named Mudd. Let's make our move." They exit the way they came, and Mark walks up behind May. "Aria Stanzer. It's Mark Right and Steve Love from the photo shoot. We're not as dead as we looked." He motions toward a refrigerator two appliances down, and Steve slides his battered rifle over the top of it. Mark pulls the letter opener from his pocket. "I'm cutting you loose. As soon as Steve plugs machine-gun boy, jump down and push this dishwasher toward me." As the last rope is cut,

Steve fires, and, realizing the rifle is finished, tosses it away. The slug penetrates the helmet and the Sergei's head. The KEP is a fine piece of protective equipment but it is not bulletproof, so the target drops to the floor. Aria jumps down, pulls off her gag, and pushes while Mark pulls creating an opening. "Hello girls." He shouts, entering the compound.

He hands his rifle to July as February tackles him with a passionate hug. "Corporal, lead them out of here. Go back to the waterfall."

"Let's go, girls."

Steve runs to the machine gun. He sees Aria's whip lying at the base and tosses it to her. "Sorry I had to put a hole in your helmet."

"It was worth it," yells Aria. "And that creep can keep it."

Steve swings the gun around and fires at the vodka drinkers, sending them inside Bolsheviky. Stalin jumps up from the throne, dumping October on the ground. "Wow! I've always wanted to shoot one of these." He fires again, blasting the toilet to bits. Stalin drags October inside as Steve makes kindling of the throne.

Mark looks at Miss February. "Charging a guy with a grenade, really?"

"You haven't seen anything yet."

"I've seen a lot."

"There's so much more." February unleashes her

mesmerizing smile.

"Help get the girls out of here."

"I'm staying with you."

"We'll be right behind you, I promise." He hands her the letter opener.

February briefly pulls her top up. "Remember, you're fighting for these."

"I love this country." He turns toward Steve. "How does that gun feel?"

"Fantastic, roadie," he sends a blast into the Bolsheviky window, destroying the large picture of Stalin. "This is a great day! I'm walking the earth and shooting at commies! Hey Stalin, you want to surrender?"

Stalin sticks his head out. "I never surrender to stupid American about to run out of bullets."

"Run out of bullets? I don't think so." He shreds Lenin's picture and then click … click … click. Marcus! I've run out of bullets, and I don't see anymore."

"Fuck. To the golf cart!" The two dash toward the cart as the Sergeis fire at them. One bullet singes Steve's beard as they jump on the conveyance—luckily, the key is in the ignition—and speed away with Steve rubbing his chin. "That was a close shave."

"Damn," Mark rues. "I thought we had that commie bastard."

"And that commie bitch bastard," sneers Steve.

"Her too. Inside every leftist is a communist

waiting to come out."

"Remember when you write your screenplay that the good guys never run out of bullets."

"Noted."

"Hey, Dude, I think February is crazy about you."

"I don't even know her real name. I mean, women have given me fake names before, but this seems different."

"My third wife never gave me her real name until our fifth date."

"You should have dumped her."

"I should have, but she had a really fast Mustang, and I was driving a shitty Honda."

"Steve, you are too good an American to drive a Honda."

"That's why I wanted the Mustang. This cart is faster than that Honda."

"With that in mind. Step on it!"

He accelerates just as a large metal wall slides out of the right side of the mall and into their path. Steve hits the brakes but they slam into it and ... blackout.

CHAPTER 10
A Terrible Lizard and an Old Familiar Stench

Outside the employee entrance the media circus continues, and the wavy-haired reporter from WDOA is doing a live shot. "Despite the commotion that threatened his beloved mall, Nelson Trafalgar took time out to declare that he was, in fact, gay."

Suddenly, Burley Dick's car swerves into the parking lot and smashes into the rear of the WDOA live truck, causing the mast to break and land on a nearby power line that the truck should have been set up far away from. A ball of deadly energy engulfs the reporter. The cameraman, a stocky ne'er-do-well named Cal, who still wears his faded high school football jersey number 00, (certainly not a comment on his intelligence), runs away. "Oh... Fuck..." screams the word slinger, as his hair fries and the makeup crackles off of his face.

Burley Dick staggers out of his car. "Watch your mouth. The FCC will fine us for that, and it will come out of your paycheck."

"My... hair..."

Burley is approached by a stereotypical Irish cop, seldom seen this side of a 1940s Warner Brothers sound stage. "What be your business here, me laddie?"

Burley points toward the mall. "Two of my employees are G.O.I.T., goofing off in there."

"Do I be smelling liquor on your breath?"

"That's medication. For my condition."

"Aye. I have a few such conditions me-self." With his right index finger, the cop taps a flask shaped bulge pushing against the inside of his right hip pocket.

"I have to get inside there and fire those two."

"That mall be sealed up tighter than the Madonna's private parts. So, stand back or I'll be bustin' ya upside the head with me shillelagh. In fact, all of you need to be takin' a few steps back toward the Emerald Isle."

Once again, stereotypes are funny and, in this case, possibly hallucinatory. Burley looks down at the extra crispy reporter. "F.Y.H. Fix your hair. You're representing the entire WDOA team."

But, for this reporter, it is too late. His hair is destroyed. He was in line to be promoted to anchor but will now have to go work in a bottom ten market. Idaho is likely in his future.

Back inside in front of Bolsheviky, Mark wakes

up to find himself sitting on the curb along Catgrass Creek with his back toward the store and his feet on the creek bank. He tries to straighten up but realizes his hands are tied to his ankles by a single strand of rope. He sees his friend in the same position just to his left. "Steve … Steve…"

Steve comes around, trying to force his hands loose to no avail. "Oh, man. What happened, Dude?"

"We were knocked out again."

"Now I know what Joe Mannix always felt like."

"And I think we're captured."

"Well, Marcus, it's still a hell of a day at work."

"That much is certain."

"Ah, now I remember, Spock from *Star Trek 4*."

Ivan comes up behind them, having heard their conversation. "Who is this Spock? We soon capture him too." Mark and Steve strain their necks to look back at him.

"You won't get him. He's dead again," Mark says. "And this time, he hasn't come back."

"I capture him. Then, I find cow and sex it up." He grabs a Stalin mug off the top of a dryer and dips vodka from a replacement toilet quickly scavenged by the Sergeis.

"Steve, I think we've been captured by a *Saturday Night Live* skit. Back from when it was still funny, not the current version."

"That much is certain."

"I meant to tell you, Steve, that movie you like was on the other night."

"Which one's that?"

"*From Here to Eternity.*"

"Great movie, bro."

"We don't disagree on much, but I don't like it."

"Really?"

"I give you that the attack on Pearl Harbor part is interesting but everyone in the thing is a dumbass. I mean Burt Lancaster doing the commanding officer's wife. Dumbass. Frank Sinatra deserting his post and getting locked up under the guy that wants to kill him. Dumbass. And that boxer idiot. He endures all that torture because he doesn't want to fight. All he had to do was join the team, rake in the perks and then take a dive in his first fight. Then he gets shot trying to sneak back onto the base while it's on high alert, when he could have just walked up to the front gate and told them he got caught off base during the attack, was wounded by flying glass, and got laid up for a while."

"I never thought of it like that."

"Then that scene on the beach when Burt Lancaster is rolling around with that chick. All you see is his nasty body. You barely see her wet butt or anything."

Stalin walks out of the storefront and up to the trashcan just behind Mark and Steve. The top of the trashcan has been used to sort the contents of their pockets. He is followed by October with the soviet history book under her arm. She sneers at them. "Hello, losers. Meet a real man." She pats Stalin on the butt. Steve and Mark twist their bodies to get a better look.

"Hello, traitor," Mark shoots back. "That red bikini on a little too tight?"

Stalin picks up the letter opener that was in Steve's pocket. "Knife with funny head very sharp. Perhaps I use it to cut off your dicks."

"Let me do it, Joey," pleads October.

"You just want to see a big one after looking at his," cajoles Mark.

Stalin reads the pair's drivers licenses. "Mark Right. Steve Love."

Steve is outraged. "Dude! You picked our pockets."

"Stalin!" yells Mark. "Where's your vaccine card?"

"Fuck vaccine card."

"At least we agree on that."

"You two rich Americans have total of eight dollars and twenty-nine cents between yourselves."

"We work in TV," Steve adds.

"I do not know this TV of which you speak, but I will find it and destroy it."

"WDOA is already destroying TV without your help," broadcasts Steve.

Mark seizes the moment as he twists toward Stalin even more to get a good look back at the mighty ass.

"Stalin, look me in the eye and say: 'You're just a stupid policeman, Mr. Bond.'"

"Your Yankee humor is nothing to us. In the revolution, we have no humor."

Mark sees Trotsky emerging to join the group. "What about Trotsky's goatee?"

"I beg your pardon?"

"You guys do know that you're not in your time period," states Mark.

Trotsky tries to answer. "Something curious is…"

"The time is of no meaning," interrupts Stalin. "In every time, I am the mighty ass of Bolshevism."

"Hail to the mighty ass!" screams October.

"Dude!" laughs Steve. "You call yourself the mighty ass?"

"Soon, I call you two, dead asses." He slides their driver's licenses into his pocket.

Mark sees the book October is carrying. "Trotsky. I bet there's a lot of books in there. Have you looked at any? Find a biography of you and one of Stalin. Which one is thinner?"

Stalin jumps in while Trotsky ponders. "Books are for the burning and not reading. The people of the revolution will not be taught how to read. I will tell them how they should think."

Mark nods to the Stalin mugs on top of the dryer. "Trotsky, is there a mug with your face on it in there?"

Stalin continues. "Mugs are for the drinking

of wonderful vodka, not for looking at handsome picture."

"Hey Stalin," asks Steve. "These ropes hurt. How about loosening them ol' commie buddy of mine?"

"Maybe I take them off."

"Yeah."

"And put them around your neck." Stalin grabs his throat to emphasis the point.

"Forget it. I'm good."

"Now, you two off jerks cause me some trouble. You kill my Sergeis and upset my Sergeis."

"Really?" asks Steve. "They're all named Sergei?"

"I be Ivan."

"Congratulations, bro."

A vodka swirling Sergei steps over to glower at Mark and Steve. "Sergei is dead. Sergei is dead. Sergei is dead. Sergei is dead…"

"And that Sergei I smashed in the face isn't looking too good," smiles Mark.

"So, you see I must recruit new men," announces Stalin.

Mark fears what is coming. "Oh, no. No. No. No."

"I am sure you know comrade Barger of spoons."

Garmon steps out from the store front wearing his CCCP warm-ups and kicking a piece of throne out of his path.

"Hello idiots. I see you are all tied up at the moment." He takes a device from his pocket and shows it to Mark. "I have security devices all over the mall. With this, I was able to put that little wall in your path."

"Thanks, Looneyburger. I was afraid we were going to get away."

Stalin beams. "This is the man who will help me build up my empire as seen in book. He also very good dresser and he have partner from England who help."

"One man, two traitors," says Mark.

"Nelson and I have signed quite a contract with Mr. Stalin, and with my mall as headquarters, we will help him conquer time."

"I also have another new man."

Mark groans and yields to the inevitable. "Bring him out."

J.P. Forte struts into view with his video camera on his shoulder. "Smile assholes."

"Comrade Forte is my new minister of propped ganders."

"Propped ganders?" groans Mark. "If you're going to kill us, just do it now."

Forte explains. "I got to thinking I could goose me up some serious jack by making films for a famous dictator."

"You forgot to use a cussword in that sentence," Steve observes.

"Dick-o-rama!"

"That's better."

"Where's your tall toady Hotwad?" asks Mark.

Forte points to his left. "He's on the other side of this damned clever appliance fence polishing my knob."

"I think you've been polishing some knobs yourself."

Stalin scratches his ass as October sidles up to him. "Mighty ass, I love reading in this book how you won the great war all by yourself."

Mark and Steve decide to taunt with Steve leading off. "Hey, mighty ass, you creeps had some help in that war."

"I don't see how you Bolsheviks ever made it in the war with your poor fashion sense."

"You might have beaten the Germans, with a lot of help, but they had better uniforms," laughs Steve.

"They won the best dressed award at the post-war banquet," Mark guffaws.

"Shut it up, you bastard faced fucks."

"Whoa! More good shit." Forte sets down his camera and writes in his notebook."

Ivan goes to the toilet for a refill and notices small ripples starting to form in the bowl as a distant thud … thud … thud is heard. He looks in the direction of the sound and screams, "*Chort*!" before running away, jumping over the northern appliance wall and knocking Hotwad down in the process.

It seems that one of the T-Rexes has grown tired

of the food warehouse and is out for a stroll along the east bank of the creek. The noise increases as the two toilet Sergeis jump over the wall trampling the prone Hotwad. "Smashed face Sergei," not seeing well, crosses the creek, emerges in front of the southeast wall and heads toward the dinosaur.

"What's going on Mark?" Steve asks.

"I think a T-Rex is coming, Steve."

"You know, I'm not surprised. At least it's not a Morlock.

"Prickland express!" shouts Forte. "I've got to get me a shot of this mofo."

"Spooner of Garmons," yells Stalin. "Why you have big lizard in your place?"

"Because he's too cheap to hire an exterminator," yells Mark.

"This is a new one on me, but no worries." Garmon pushes a button on his device and the floor slides open, revealing a staircase. "Mr. Stalin, Miss October, Mr. Forte—down here."

Stalin pushes Trotsky to the ground. "Bronstein, fight the lizard. Save the revolution." He disappears down the stairs with October. Garmon motions Forte over. As Forte starts to descend, he sees the bruised Hotwad staring at him from behind a dishwasher that is a low point in the northwest fence.

"Hotwad. Save my awards, you long-haired bitch." He goes down the stairs with Garmon and the door slides shut, crushing a piece of throne that briefly sticks in the glide path.

"Trotsky," yells Mark. "Untie us." Trotsky screams and runs away. Hurdling over the dishwasher and knocking Hotwad down again.

"Chickenshit, Bolshevik!" shouts Steve.

"He was really a Menshevik anyway," Mark points out as the threat nears.

Smashed face Sergei reaches the approaching monster and is devoured while the bound brace watch.

"Oh, that was horrible, Marcus. And he was a bad guy. I think we're screwed."

"He's kind of reddish-brown, Steve. I always thought they would be green."

"Didn't you see those movies?"

"That was silly Hollywood crap. Spielberg didn't know what color they were. He's not as big a genius as he thinks he is.

"I think this one is about to color us dead, dude."

"He sure smells bad. I guess no one's ever smelled one before now."

Steve sniffs. "That's terrible. It's hard to describe too."

"Maybe it smells like Nan Carpy taking a bath in spoiled sauerkraut."

"Wow, Mark, as much as I hate her, that's pretty erotic."

Mark looks down between his legs. "Steve! I've

got a big blue rock between my legs!"

"You really should see a doctor for that, bro."

"Larry's Bowie knife! We're in his backyard!"

"Praise, Jesus!

Mark works his heels behind the rock and pushes hard sliding it away from him. "The knife's here!" He painfully maneuvers and gets his right hand on the handle, then flips the blade sharp side up and starts cutting the rope from the bottom. "It's still sharp." The monster stops at the southeast appliance wall, but Mark still feels its hot breath. He frees himself and quickly cuts Steve loose. "I'm glad they only used one strand on us." He tosses the knife at the giant freak. Since he has never thrown a knife before, the blade wobbles around during its flight and embeds itself in the T-Rex's left nostril handle first, blade protruding. "Great. Now he's a knife nose. Steve go help protect the girls."

"What are you going to do?"

"I'll try to lead this sucker somewhere and hopefully find something to kill him with. Then I'll look for some new pants."

Steve's phone rings from the trashcan. "Really?" With a strange sense of cellular duty, he jerks it out and sees that Burley Dick is calling. "Dick, I'm kind of busy right now."

"Love, just wait till I get in there." The dinosaur roars. "Don't make that noise at me."

Steve tosses the phone into the mouth of the menace. "Dick, can you hear me now?"

"Go Steve," yells Mark. Steve collects the pair's money from the top of the trashcan then hurdles over the dishwasher knocking Hotwad down in the process. The determined lackey jumps back up and climbs over the dishwasher staring blankly at the dinosaur. "When I was a kid, I had a pet lizard, but he ran away." Suddenly the panel in the floor opens, J.P. Forte runs out, pulls Hotwad in and yells as the door closes. "Other guy, I forgot this fucker owes me money. Protect my awards!"

Mark is perturbed. "All right, Forte. Your awards are toast!" The T-Rex smashes through the southeast appliance wall destroys an American flag motif portable awning in the patio section then tramples the machine gun to pieces. Mark runs down the creek past both northern appliance walls, up the west bank and grabs the handle of the awards cart. His pursuer follows and lunges at him, but Mark keeps the cart between the two. After three more lunges, the beast does a 180 and smashes the cart with his tail. Bronze Knobs and Golden Links fly everywhere. The regional Emmy is destroyed beyond all recognition. "Great job, you've done one good thing, you bastard!" Mark runs back across the creek to the east bank and sees that the security wall that stopped him and Steve earlier is still extended. He runs behind the wall as the T-Rex slams into it, stunning himself and giving the reprieved prey time to run ahead and formulate a plan.

Outside in the media compound, Biff LaFolluvette is busy. He has sent his fallen reporter off in an ambulance for emergency treatment to save his fine head of hair—it's too late. And now, Phil Veal, the WDOA general manager, has shown up demanding to do a live commentary. Mr. Veal is under the misconception that he is wise, talented, handsome and should be on television, so he does a daily bit called *What You Should Think*. Even with the wind kicking up and his curly red hair blowing around and his large ears flapping in the breeze, he is determined to go on. With the station live truck destroyed, Biff has had to buy time on a rival station's truck. Cameraman Cal is trying to line up the shot with unsolicited help from Burley Dick.

"M.H.L.G., Cal."

"What?"

"Make him look good."

"Why don't you just say that? Stand by boss."

"I'll stand him by Cal. You shouldn't even be talking to him. I'm wearing a three-piece suit. You're wearing a football jersey and need a haircut. Stand by Mr. Veal." Cal gives the countdown anyway, and Phil Veal is on the air.

"Hello friends, this is Phil Veal, the general manager

of WDOA, and this is *What You Should Think*. I am live outside the beautiful new Taj Ma-Mall. This mall was a gift to our community from two of our leading citizens, Garmon Spooneybarger and Nelson Trafalgar. But today trouble has come to this wonderful place. There are reports of gunshots, explosions and other fantastic things that seem unbelievable. Mr. Spooneybarger and Mr. Trafalgar have evacuated the facility and locked it down to protect the public."

"One matter is of even greater concern. It seems that the famous local director and videographer J.P. Forte and his brilliant assistant, Hotwad, may be trapped inside. This is beyond disturbing. Mr. Forte is so talented. I just love his commercials for Young Bucks sausage. I have broken bread often with J.P., and I can tell you that he is nothing but a class act and a perfect gentleman. As for Hotwad, what can you say about a genius. This man has degrees from three Ivy League colleges and still found time to be a basketball star at each one, leading the league in rebounding. You seldom run across this level of brilliance."

Nan Carpy runs into the shot, hands him a note, smiles at the camera and runs out.

"I have just been given an update. Two minor WDOA employees, Steve Right and Mark Love are also trapped inside. I do not know these two, but they are part of the WDOA team, and I am confident they are safely hiding in a corner with J.P. Forte and Hotwad fighting to protect them from harm.

Now for something stunning. There are reports that time itself has been disrupted inside the mall. Dinosaurs have been spotted … T-Rexes in fact. This appears unbelievable, but if they are here, they must be welcomed into our Lewisburg neighborhoods because we are a welcoming town. If they happen to eat one of us now and then that is a small price to pay for the vibrancy and diversity that they will bring to enrich our lives."

Nan Carpy runs in and out of the shot with another note.

"Friends, this is even more fantastic. Josef Stalin, our friend and ally from World War ll, has been sighted inside. If this is true, imagine what sage advice and wise council kindly old Uncle Joe can give us. Any of us would be honored to meet him, shake his hand and thank him for saving us in that great war."

"All in all, an incredible day in our community. It seems that a new world order has descended upon us and WDOA will be here to help you conform to it. I'm Phil Veal, and this is *What You Should Think*."

"You're clear, boss," yells Cal.

"You're clear, boss," yells Burley Dick.

Phil Veal puts a Lucky Strike in his mouth and Nan Carpy shoots in to light it. "Great job, Mr. Veal. You are such a fantastic general manager. I write letters to the owner every day telling them what a great job you are doing."

"Thanks, Nan. Just keep those goddamned lizards out of our part of town, right?"

"You said it, boss."

"If Stalin is here, I would sure like to talk to him about personnel management."

"He knew how to handle people. That's for sure."

"Do you know those two guys that work for us?"

"Yeah. They're not important."

"Maybe a dinosaur will eat them." He breaks out laughing as Nan, Cal and Burley join in.

Inside, Mark stands in front Taco Tormento with a five-gallon bucket of tacos and burritos that he slopped together in the deserted kitchen. His hands are burning a little, since he violated the health code and made the items without rubber gloves. There is a lot on his mind. He wonders if he should just have just filled the bucket with ingredients rather than actually making (albeit rather poorly) the tacos and burritos. Naw, it will be fun throwing them at the beast. He hopes the food is as bad as he heard, and that it will kill the creature. He is glad that he has never worked in fast food. He ponders if he really has a girlfriend and if he should ask what her name is. He thinks back to being a kid and liking the dinosaur logo on the Sinclair gasoline signs (that one was green). Of course, that was a depiction of a plant eater, and Mark is facing a meat eater. But did eating plants give those prehistoric vegetarians tremendous gas?

As his pursuer comes into view, he hears Steve yelling out 20 yards behind him. "Mark are you alright?"

"Yeah. It's supper time for our friend. Are the girls safe?"

"We've got them inside the art store. Those ugly paintings should scare him off."

"Maybe I can kill him first."

"Good luck."

The big ugly is now 25 feet away and Mark hurls his first burrito, which misses badly. "That's why I got cut from the baseball team." With the scale-meister closer, a taco is hurled that knocks the knife out of his nose followed by a burrito that hits him in the eye which causes an open mouth roar that Mark fills with his rancid projectiles. The T-Rex starts chewing. "Damn, I think he likes Taco Tormento." Upon the next open mouth opportunity, the whole bucket is tossed in and chomped on sending plastic shards flying. Time for the secret weapon. Mark picks up a container that he had standing by. It is a jug of Taco Tormento's special ghost pepper salsa. This should be fatal. The mouth opens, the jug flies in and the nasty one seems to savor it, ducking down and inserting his head into the taco store looking for more and eating the diary of Jose Enrique de la Pena just because it's there. Mark picks up the bowie knife and runs across the creek, ending up in front of the art store where Steve, February, and July are standing guard. "Hi honey, I'm home," Mark says to February.

"What did you bring me?"

Larry's knife is handed over to her. "A used bowie knife. It once saved a couple of guys' lives."

"Just what I wanted. It's a lot better than that letter opener."

"Here comes your buddy, bro," warns Steve.

Mark looks at July. "Corporal, take your shot." She fires off two shots. One enlarges the T-Rex's right nostril the second removes his left ear. The blustering beast does not notice either one and continues running toward Mark, who ducks into The Gift of the Elvi with one thought—*the kitsch in here alone should kill him*. Rex lowers his body and tries to auger his way in as Mark bounces a couple of toilet seats off his nose. July fires two shots into his back, and February cuts a hunk of his hide off with the knife.

Steve has done a quick look inside the classic sports shop and found one golf club; a nine-iron signed by Erin Nordegren, the ex-wife of Tiger Woods. He swiftly utilizes it to pound on the beast's backside, to little avail. In the store, the freak inches closer as Mark runs out of toilet seats. "Listen, lizard, I bet Stalin's fat ass would taste a lot better than my skinny one." He picks up a milk chocolate Elvis bust and bounces it off the bleeding nose. "You're busted, Dino bitch!" The mouth opens wide, and the stench of the breath is overpowering. "You Jurassic jerks ever heard of mouthwash?" Mark looks around and picks up a jar of peanut butter and 'nanner spread. "This should do the trick." The jar is pitched deep into the rancid throat and Mark waits. "Anytime, now. Come on. Die, you bastard!" Ignoring his prey for a moment, Dino boy chows down on the tabletop where the jars of the dubious spread sit. "Fuck! That killed him in the first draft!"

Minutes later, the pursuit continues with the frustrated slayer and his attacker running around food trucks, as Steve continues to pound on the big lizard's back and February neuters him with a deft move and ponders briefly if she should have become a veterinarian. Mark jumps into a small café and recognizes an old putrid smell from long ago. A smell even worse than the dinosaur breath. "No, it can't be." He looks around, and on a table set up for an unfinished meal sits a bowl of French cut green beans. "I don't believe it. I thought Spooney was joking." Quickly, the gaping mouth is upon him, and he sails the bowl into it like a Frisbee. Expecting more Taco Tormento or peanut butter and 'nanner spread, the growling gourmet bites down on something that he and his ilk had avoided in the food warehouse. He backs out into the walkway making strange noises. "Gggerkkk!

Gaaaaak! Griiikkkk! Groonnkkkk!" Then he falls over dead with a thud that registers on the seismograph at the University of Lewisburg. "Son of a bitch!" Mark searches the kitchen and finds a partial case of the green menace now packaged in glass bottles and called Le Slice.

As Steve and February inspect the carcass, Mark approaches them carrying the case. "Bro! How did you do it?" wonders Steve.

He tosses Steve a jar. "It was French cut green beans that killed the beast. They're packaged nicer but are just like we remember. Garmon brought them here out of spite, and they saved me. I never thought I would say this, but I love the smell of French cut green beans in the morning. It smells like victory."

"You guys have a history with these beans?" February wonders.

"Steve likes to throw them at girls. I use them to kill dinosaurs. We'll take these with us. He might have some friends."

February puts her arm around Mark. It's good to have friends."

"For humans, yes. For dinosaurs, let's hope not."

CHAPTER 11
Let's Make Some Fossil Fuel

B iff LaFolluvette is frustrated. It's not just the fact that he can't go live with his own equipment, thanks to the drunken idiot Burley Dick, but the other stations seem to be finding exclusive interviews with people who have just exited the mall. Then he spots it. Just to the left of the employee entrance, hidden by the portable toilets, is an open window. It seems that the metal plate positioned above it failed to engage, and fleeing mall patrons have broken out the glass and are trickling out. And climbing out into his line of sight are Abraham Lincoln and George Washington Carver who seem to be having a tiff. Knowing he will need something great to buy more live time, he thinks this is it.

"President Lincoln, I've never seen a white guy run as fast as you did from that dinosaur."

"Carver, your little peanut legs were moving pretty fast too."

Biff tries to seize the moment. "Hey guys. How about an interview? Tell us what's going on inside there."

"What station are you with, sir?" asks Abe.

"WDOA, Channel 82."

"I am the President of the United States, and I think I deserve a higher rated media outlet."

"And I, George Washington Carver, cannot waste time talking about my peanuts on the number four station."

"G.W.C., I think I see a better station set up right over there."

"Let's go, Mr. President."

"Pricks!" Biff shouts after them as he turns to look in the window. The employee alcove is lined with food kiosks and fifty yards away a Tyrannosaurus Rex is eating the Chick Filet stand. "Holy fuck. Cal, get over here with your camera!"

Cameraman Cal responds at a leisurely pace. "What's up, boss?"

"Look in there."

"Whoa … I'll zoom in and get a shot."

"No, you've got to climb in there and get up real close. He's eating and won't even notice you."

"That's crazy, boss."

"A real close shot will get me an Emmy."

"Can I get an Emmy too?"

"You can touch mine."

"Forget that shit." He tosses the camera to Biff and disappears at a less than leisurely pace.

"Jerk! I'll just do it myself." After a struggle, Biff makes it through the casement. A nearly naked Cleopatra runs past him and jumps through the opening with ease. "Put some pants on, bitch!" Now he turns his attention to the camera. "This can't be too hard. Steve Love can run one."

Twenty yards in Biff is noticed by the T-Rex who immediately charges. "Oh, fuck!" The fat flee-er gets stuck during his attempted egress. The dinosaur takes a bite out of his ass then swings his tail, shooting the news director out of the window, his toupee sailing off, and in the direction of the porta-cans, which he smashes into sending pieces of blue plastic, chemicals, noxious substances and camera all about just as, activated by the commotion, the steel plate slams shut over the window.

"Mr. LaFolluvette, are you all, right?" Calls out Nan Carpy.

Cal is less sympathetic. "Hey guy, you broke my camera, and you smell like shit."

"I'll find your hair and get something for your butt, boss."

"Thanks, Nan. Fuck you, Cal."

In front of the art store, Mark is giving a lecture on how to kill dinosaurs with the French cut green beans. He has an attentive audience, except for Miss

August, who has wandered off into the atrium and Miss June, who is inside touching herself in front of some more Hunter Biden paintings. It's a damned shame that the guy is so prolific. "These beans should kill them, but I still wish we could get in that gun store." He points to the locked steel door.

January steps forward pulling a pin from her hair. "I can probably open that. My grandfather is always locking himself out of our family restaurant, and he insists on having the only key which he frequently loses. Since I live nearby, he calls me to break in for him."

"How did you learn that skill?" Mark asks.

"Ancient American secret." She takes a step toward the gun store, but everyone's attention is diverted when Biff's friend, who has advanced quickly and quietly up Catgrass Creek, barely making a splash in the shallow water, zips out onto the west bank and zeros in on August pursuing her around the atrium. This causes Steve to think fast.

"They're attracted to blue. Take off your top."

August unfastens her blue bandeau and tosses it in the air releasing her two huddled masses who were yearning to breathe free. The T-Rex catches it with his little arm, sniffs it and eats it. "What a pervert," says August. Seemingly pleased, the creature sits down with his mouth open looking lovingly at her. This allows for Steve to slide over and toss in the bean bomb, ending this budding relationship as the reptile Romeo falls over on his back dead. Stax bounces over to Steve with her exposed passengers enjoying the trip and gives him a crushing hug and a very wet kiss. "My hero, thank you."

"You're welcome, Mam ... eries." He jumps on the stomach of the dead critter. "I'm king of the world."

Mark looks up at his friend. "How did you know they were attracted to blue?"

"I didn't."

June joins the group and eyes the carcass. "Like, you shouldn't have killed him. Dinosaurs are people too."

Ten female voices ring out in unison. "Shut up, bitch."

"I'll get on that door now," says January.

The *Titanic* crewman shoots out of the south wing. "Dinosaurs! Dinosaurs, dead ahead!"

"I guess I'll wait."

Three more T-Rexes are zipping up the creek toward the group. July seizes the moment and takes charge.

"Mark, Steve, take a break. The calendar team will handle this."

"Not me," huffs June as she clip-clops away on her six-inch heels, adjusting her French cut bottom.

"Forget that bitch. Which of you can throw?"

"Gardening biceps," chirps April.

"Seven years on the library softball team," points out March.

"I've thrown things at boyfriends for years," yells September.

July tosses jars of beans to April, March, and September. All right, we're going to have three squads of three. One tosser and two tormentors in each group. Squad one is March, August and December. Squad two September, November and February. Squad three, April, January and May. Our mission is to harass these bastards and get that jar in their mouth."

The beasts enter the atrium, and the girls fan out choosing their prey. "This should be good roadie," Steve says to Mark.

July shouts out orders as the action intensifies. "Left side, three. Get on it, two. Go. Go. Go one. Let's put these bitches down."

Squad one is hitting it hard. December kicks a dent in a scaly leg with her red boots. "You remind me of my last date except your breath is better." August squeezes her bare boobs at the creature. "Hey, pervert, you want these? Yeah, you want them."

The T-Rex under attack by squad three is getting weak in the knees as January chops away at his left. "Bitch, I'll cut you up for the lunch buffet tomorrow." And May unloads the whip on his right. "Taste the whip, you ugly-assed mo-fo."

Hiding behind the elevator shaft, Stalin watches

the action munching on a tub of popcorn salvaged by one of his Sergeis. "This stuff not bad for watching naked American women fight big lizards."

Squad two is about to claim the first scalp as November steps on a foot. "You should have worn your steel toed shoes." And February sticks in the bowie knife. "You're about to feel a little prick, you big prick." September gets her shot and tosses the jar in. "Mmm, mmm, dead!"

Squad one is next as April gets off a throw. "Better ingredients. Deader dinosaur."

Last, but just as lethal, number three gets the job done as April plants her beans. "Whore-is, it's time for your din-din." The three Jurassic jerks drop one after another. The three squads of slayers high five one another. Steve looks at Mark. "That's the hottest thing I have ever seen."

"And they had good one-liners," answers Mark. "That's important for a big action scene." Suddenly a sixth T-Rex powers out of the south wing and makes a quick left turn as if he has heard about the slayers and doesn't want any part of them. Mark is closest to the dwindling case of beans and gets off a throw that bounces off a closed mouth.

There are six jars of beans left. Steve, Mark and February each take two jars and offer chase. The dinosaur has stopped at a food truck called Butt Boys. Why must all pork trucks have attempts at cute names? He knocks the truck on its side, eats the plastic pig on top, rips open the side, consumes the expensive inventory and an authentic "Butt Boy" who was hiding inside. Now, with a wide-open mouth, he turns to stare at his pursuers, Steve and February send jars flying, the mouth clamps shut, and the jars bounce off smashing to pieces on the floor.

The mouth opens again, Mark throws, the mouth closes in time. This T-Rex seems to have figured things out. Suddenly, Aria Stanzer runs at him screaming. She quickly jumps up on the pork truck and onto the dinosaur's back, holding on with her left hand and pounding his head with the whip in her right.

"That takes a lot of guts," observes February.

"Let's hope we don't see them." counters Mark.

May spins her mount around in a circle with his mouth open. February fires a shot but the tricky beast still clams up in time. The mouth opens again, and Steve, mesmerized by the sight of a nearly naked female jockey with black boots whipping a Tyrannosaurus Rex, misses his throw badly.

Mark holds the last jar in his hand. There are more in the food warehouse, but that's a mile away. "Excuse me," says a voice, and the trio turns to see a good looking, black haired young man in a Brooklyn Dodgers uniform. "I am not sure what is going on. I was walking around the field after the game and ended up here. I strolled around for a bit and found this sports store. I don't know why anyone would want to buy that stuff. Then a war broke out and it seemed like a good place to shelter. Now it looks like you need to kill this…uh…dinosaur, that is ridden by a very attractive young lady, with a jar of some kind of green beans. Perhaps I can help."

Mark tosses the jar to the man. He weighs it in his left hand. "Aria, point him this way." She spins him toward the group of four with his mouth tightly closed. The young man unleashes a blazing rocket that smashes through the dino's teeth, sears his tongue, scorches his throat and breaks open inside his stomach. The Tyrannosaurus starts rocking back and forth, and Aria Stanzer leaps to safety as he drops dead.

"Great throw, sir," Mark says.

"Happy to help," replies the man rubbing his left elbow. "I'm getting better with my control."

February hugs Aria, which gets the attention of Mark and Steve.

Steve turns to Mark. "I guess this guy bought one of those jerseys."

"I don't think he had to buy one. It's the T-Rex who bought it."

Miss June clip-clops over. "I'm left-handed, too, but I don't kill things."

"Get lost!" yells May as she smacks June on the ass with the whip.

Steve thinks to himself, *I have to get me one of those whips.*

Mark thinks to himself, *I have to get me one of those whips.*

Miss February thinks to herself, *I bet both Mark and Steve would like to get one of those whips.*

Stax Spankster, who has a vast knowledge of baseball history, runs up to the young man with a magic marker borrowed from the art store. "That was a great throw. Would you autograph my right breast?"

"This is a most unusual day," replies the perplexed man.

"I love this country," smiles Steve.

CHAPTER 12
A Powerful Stream and Two Stainless Steel Beauties

In the one hour that has passed since the last Tyrannosaurus Rex tasted the west wing green bean diet and dropped dead, a lot has happened. The injured and dead around the atrium needed to be dealt with, so a hospital was set up in the Bed, Bath & Beyond with a morgue in the art shop for the murdered citizens. The B, B & B had already closed in the short time since the mall opened because of the bad corporate decision to stop stocking Mike Lindell's fine products, but the space was still full of inferior sheets and towels to dab wounds and cover up bodies.

The makeshift nursing staff consisted of Miss September who spent a quarter in nursing school before switching to business college, Miss April who often taught a first aid class on how to treat common gardening injuries, and Miss March who sometimes sat in on first aid classes offered at the library including one's taught by Miss April. The new friend from Brooklyn pitched in on the retrieval effort then excused himself to do some exploring. The two security guys showed up to help, announcing that Garmon had fired them, and introduced themselves as Bob and Chuck, which Mark had a vague memory of in the back of his mind. The casualty count was 12 injured and 17 dead. This was a bill that the Bolsheviks had rung up and one they must pay for, as there were still 19 Sergeis, Ivan, Trotsky, Miss October, and Stalin to be dealt with along with their two new friends.

Lumina's Salsa Bar situated just the other side of the B, B & B suffered no dinosaur damage, so November requested that January take a break from her lock breaching attempt so they could whip up some delicious crepes for everyone. Although June requested only three green olives for her meal and was mocked by September for racism against black olives. July came along to use the phone in the salsa bar to contact a friend of hers who was on the Lewisburg SWAT team. He told her that they had been milling around the mall's main entrance for hours with Garmon and Nelson refusing to answer their calls and police leadership indecisive about blowing the doors and coming in. She told him about the wounded, described what the bad guys would look like and what the good people were wearing, many of them not much. She also told him that the good side may have weapons when they entered, as she expected that a breach of the gun store lock was eminent, and informed him of a few dead surprises laying around.

The lunch was enjoyed by all except June who consumed her three olives as if holding a grudge against the very notion of food and August who seems to have wandered off after using her bare breasts to bring a smile to the faces of several wounded men. Columbus rambled by and was offered a crepe with ranch dressing which he happily accepted and consumed before continuing his journey. The security duo tells Mark that Stalin, October and J.P. Forte are in the manor house, but they don't know where any of the other men are. Mark figures they will make a play for the time portal and hopes the good guys get inside the gun store soon.

Stax Spankster approaches the group carrying an armful of tops she has collected from Victoria's Secret and other women's stores. She has decided to cover up a little but not much as she enjoys the half-naked feel and has eschewed the notion of a shirt a decision that will benefit any future movie version of this novel. She pops on a pink bra and looks for comments from her cohorts.

"Too bedroom," says January as she walks back

to the gun store lock.

She changes to a white top.

"Too virgin for you," laughs March as she frees her hair from the top of her head and shakes it down around her shoulders, which gets the attention of Steve.

A leather top is donned.

"Lesbo city," states September. "Unless you're into that." She winks and blows Stax a kiss.

A fringed number is quickly displayed.

"Musical theatre," sings April, stretching her arms out and dropping to her knees.

Earth tone is tried next.

"Too migrant," judges November.

Now a black spandex top is twisted on.

"Not bad," notes February. "If you were Batgirl."

"Fuck all you bitches," steams August as she straps on a blue bandeau bikini top nearly identical to the one consumed by the perverted T-Rexer.

"Perfect," smiles Steve.

"Thank you."

Steve whispers to Mark. "Maybe another dinosaur will be attracted to blue."

Another dinosaur is about to show up, but on a different scale. Miss June has wandered over to the remains of the dinosaur trampled cell phone kiosk hoping to find a phone and call her mother to complain that everyone is being mean to her but has found all the phones crushed. She decides to wash up a little and walks to the edge of Catgrass Creek squatting down parallel to a clump of bushes. Steve spots her as she pulls down her right cup to wash her ample boob and lets out a shrill whistle of approval. She pulls the cup up and gives him the finger as, seemingly activated by the sound of the whistle, the small plant eater jumps out of a bush. He is unseen by June as she dabs her left breast.

"Look out," warns September.

"Shut up, bitch," responds June.

"OK."

"Is that a baby?" asks August.

March, ever the astute librarian has the answer. "That's a plant eater called an Albertadormeus Syntarsus. The brats that come into the library are always looking for dinosaur books, so we keep a lot of them on hand, books that is, but we have our share of brats."

The little creature swings an out-of-proportion member in the direction of June and saturates her with a urine stream. "Fuck! Fuck! Fuck!" June screams as onlookers laugh.

"Bitch, you've been pissed on by a dinosaur!" convulses September.

The urinator stops streaming, squawks and runs off with a methane release as January announces to the still laughing group that the gun store lock has finally succumbed to her labor. "We're in!" Everyone runs over to help lift the heavy door as June is left dripping in smelly urine, probably the first person to ever be pissed on by a dinosaur.

The door is quickly elevated, and January gets to unlocking the display cases. "Home again," Steve announces. "Let's get armed for battle." He gravitates to a display of Galco holsters for the hip, straps one on and hands one to Mark who follows suite. "Now we decide what to fill them up with."

"We could get a Remington and get it done or make the score Colt 45 Russian bastards nothing," suggests Mark.

"A Sig would sour their outlook, or we could embrace them with our Charter Arms," ponders Steve.

"We can get a Glock and blow off Trotsky's cock," says Mark.

"Here's the ticket, roadie," shouts Steve as he points to a display of Springfield Model 1911 pistols in stainless steel. "One of these can blow a hole thru Stalin the size of Gorky Park. Load up." They each select a gun and insert a magazine which consists of seven 45 caliber bullets. They park the guns in their holsters which are emitting a pleasant new leather smell and shove some extra mags in their back pockets.

Steve suggests that the security guys and every woman who feels comfortable with a gun get armed.

Bob selects a Sig Sauer with a DeSantis shoulder holster and Chuck grabs a Glock and an Uncle Mike's shoulder holster, then both step out to look for a conveyance. Corporal Striker trades her Nagant for an AR-15, which is a civilian version of her Army rifle. Aria Stanzer has picked out a Smith and Wesson model 29, 44 magnum and, eschewing a holster, shoves it into the right side of her micro bikini bottom, which Steve finds extremely hot. Miss February has taken a 12-gauge, camo pattern, Mossberg shotgun. She loads in five Federal shells with #4 buckshot and slips five more into the waistband of her bikini bottom which Mark finds extremely hot. Steve, Mark, and July each take a Motorola two-way radio from a convenient display.

Stax Spankster slips a small derringer into her new large top. September latches on to a Remington Wildcat .22 rifle saying it's like the one she uses every fall when she helps her uncle collect squirrels, raccoons, possums and maybe a couple of rats for his annual urban Burgoo Festival. January displays confidence in her martial arts skills, and November says she can take down any attacker with a spatula and heads to her restaurant for one. April suggests she would be more comfortable with a knife, and February hands her Larry's Bowie knife, which she had holstered in the side of her bikini bottom which, yes, Mark and Steve found to be extremely hot.

March and December pick up cans of mace. June is off somewhere still drying out. October is, of course, on the list to be dealt with.

Mark gets a thought and asks Grace Chan to open the display cases containing the rifles of Davy Crockett and Alvin York and the helmet riding crop and field glasses of General Patton. "Whoa, bro," smiles Steve. "Are you thinking…"

"I'm thinking that if that photo thing is some kind of time portal, we might be able to draft some help." He addresses Miss February. "Think you can operate a time machine?"

"Probably, I'm an electrical engineer with a master's degree and my own consulting firm."

"Of course you are. And what's the name of that firm?"

"Miss February's Electrical Consultants, L.L.C."

"You're not going to tell me your name, huh?"

"Not yet." She makes a zipping motion across her lips.

The security duo arrives in a Cushman cart with three rows of seats. Mark tosses them a two-way radio then a plan is laid out. Corporal Striker will lead the all-female security squad protecting the gun store and the makeshift hospital. Steve will scout around looking for the Bolsheviks. Mark, February, Chuck, and Bob will proceed to the holographic photo place to recruit some help.

On the trip down the south wing, Mark points out where Steve and he crashed into the steel plate. Then the crew stops near Bolsheviky to clear appliances and pieces of toilet and throne out of the path of the cart and sweep the place for commies (none are found). Mark studies the outline of the sliding panel on the floor, curses not having a way to open it, points out the blood spot across the way that was a Sergei and wishes that the machine gun had not been smashed. Then they are on their way.

Exiting the cart near the holographic photo store, a Pterodactyl shoots out of the joint directly at the quartet. The three guys unload onto this latest threat, and it glides to its demise in Catgrass Creek. Upon crossing the footbridge and entering the space, another Pterodactyl that was perched on top of the computers dives at them, and February ends its flight.

On the stage, the Jurassic countryside is still visible. February steps behind the control panel after handing her shotgun to Mark who looks thru the giant hole in the wall hoping no more T-Rexes have dropped by for a free meal. Amid a huge mess that makes the people on *Hoarders* look neat, he spots only the small Albertadormeus who has returned for a treat after dodging a sexual advance from Ivan. He tells Chuck and Bob the little guy should be left alone because he seems mostly harmless and that someone might soon be in the mall who deserves to be pissed on. Then he sends them to guard the entrance before joining February behind the control panel.

"A lot of these switches don't do anything; they're just for show. I guess the operator put on a little act."

Mark points to the stage. "Can you get rid of that scenery before we get another visitor?"

She pushes a button, and in ten seconds, the stage is blank. "There's a countdown built into the off switch. More show business."

Mark glances into the far northwest corner of the room and spots a giant, black and brown prehistoric snake coiled up from floor to ceiling and staring at him. He hands the Mossburg back to Miss February and steps behind her pointing to the snake "Can you get rid of that before I scream like Dr. Smith?"

"Whoa! That's big."

"It's a Titanoboa the largest snake to ever slither across the earth, or at least the largest one outside of Washington, D.C."

"I bet he's not bullet proof." She vaporizes the snake's head with a quick blast, sets the gun on the counter, then returns to scrolling thru a computer screen. "We know Bolsheviks, Christopher Columbus and dinosaurs are here. What other people from history have you seen?

"Lady Godiva."

"Oh, yeah, that one."

"And possibly Leonardo DaVinci, and a crewman

from the *Titanic*."

"They are all on this list. And their images were all left up for a while. So, it seems that if this thing is left on one location an active time portal is created. This is a time machine. The first one I've run into."

"There are strange legends about the land in this area. Maybe this machine is tapping into something that was already here," Mark ponders.

She points at the chandelier. "People think that crystals have a lot of power."

"Are there any cavemen on that list?"

"Yeah, that image was open for over three hours."

"Supposedly, a caveman stole a boombox here then disappeared."

"He took a blast back to the past," February laughs.

"You think you can summon us some help? I've got some dates for you."

"Sure thing. I love meeting new people."

CHAPTER 13
Reinforcements

Steve has located the enemy, warned the calendar squad, notified Mark on the radio and is near the Rocket Belt display when he spots Trotsky standing in Victoria's Secret examining a pair of panties. He creeps toward the little pervert and gets about 15 feet away without being spotted. With his hand near his weapon, he issues a command, "Trotsky! Drop those panties and get out here now!" Trotsky throws down the item of interest and steps toward Steve. "Why didn't you untie us, you son of a bitch?"

"I am too important to the revolution to risk being so near a monster."

"You little weasel, you're near a monster all the time. What the hell do you think Stalin is?"

"Stalin is a peasant, just like Khrushchev. I will handle him. I will save the revolution."

"Stalin is going to take over for Lenin, throw you out and then kill you. Khrushchev will also rule the

Soviet Union; you won't."

"I see phony mugs. They mean nothing." He points to Steve's "Don't Tread on Me" shirt. "Just like phony American Revolution, which only aided the rich."

"I should kick your ass."

"I am the People's Commissar of Military and Naval Affairs. I can have you pummeled."

"You can have me pummeled? Can you do it yourself? Have you ever been in a fight?" The two men have been inching closer to each other while they talked and are now only a couple of feet apart.

"Of course, I have been in fight. I fight all the time."

"You fight on a piece of paper. You fight to comb your hair in the morning. I'm talking about the real thing, dude, man to man. I'm from the south end of Lewisburg. I was in fights before I could walk." Steve holds his arms straight out to his sides. "Make the first move, you tweed toad." Trotsky meekly slaps him on the cheek. "That's all you got. Try again." Trotsky kicks him on the shin. "Good Lord, I'm going to have to teach you to fight before I can pound you. Lesson one is never hit a guy with glasses." He removes Trotsky's glasses with his left hand, punches him three times in the face with his right and then puts the glasses back on. "That's how you fight."

"That hurt."

"Of course, and this is going to hurt more," Steve

repeats the maneuver. "Don't cry, fight back." The diminutive Bolshevik charges as Steve puts him in a headlock. They twirl around, and their inertia carries them down the creek bank into the shallow drink. Trotsky gets loose and tries to pull Steve's hair but cannot get a grip. His glasses fall off as Steve pounds away putting only one thought in the commie's head.

"This water will not be good for my imported French shoes."

"Dude, you are pathetic. What girl's school did you go to anyway?" Their momentum is stopped as they come up against one of the concrete boulders with the 20-foot falls stretching out below them. The People's Commissar tries to knee Steve in the testicles, but the two simultaneously slip and start dropping. Next stop is the Lewisburg sewer system. They fall side-by-side, and at the two-foot mark, Steve punches Trotsky.

Four feet down. Steve punches Trotsky.

Six feet. Steve punches Trotsky.

Eight feet. Steve punches Trotsky twice.

At the 10-foot mark, they pass the sub-atrium floor. Only ten more feet to go. Mr. Love punches his adversary again as a leather strap flies in front of his own face. He grabs it, stopping his fall. The little Commissar continues downward, swirls around the collection pool and disappears into the sewer system, leaving behind an echo of ((("Oyyyyyy ...

Veyyyyy!!"))) "Most satisfying flush I've ever had," states Steve as he realizes the leather strap is pulling him upward. He grabs the shaky rail and climbs over to discover that the strap is one of the reins of Lady Godiva's horse upon which she sits smiling at him, pleased that she has pulled him to safety. "Oh, hello," he beams. "I was hoping to run into you again."

She slides off her silk blanket and walks over to him, her heels clicking on the marble floor. The Coventry cutie squeezes his butt with her right hand and coos, "the passion."

At the holographic photo store, Miss February is about to call up the Alamo on the morning of March 6, 1836, when the operator of the machine returns quite the worse for wear. "Hello, strangers touching my equipment."

"So, you work here?" asks Mark.

"Yeah, I'm Nate. What the hell is going on?"

"You have a time machine here."

"That explains those dinosaurs. I ran away when I saw them, then I thought I should come back and warn people, but the Taco Tormento kicked in and the porta-cans were smashed, so I just went in a wrecked car that was out there. It was an electric car that was leaking battery acid, didn't think my contribution would matter much.

"You must be a deep thinker," says Mark.

Nate continues, "Even though the mall was on

lockdown, I tried the service door, which was open because the steel plate had not engaged. I came in and tapped on the plate. It closed, and here I am."

"That's a fascinating story," mocks February. "We were about to call up some help, do you mind?"

"To kill the dinosaurs?"

"We already killed them. We're after Bolsheviks now."

"Go right ahead. I'm not paid enough to run a time machine. I could even sit in the back."

"Stay out here; you might be useful," orders Mark.

"Nate," says February. "I've taken all of your BS out of the board, so it should work fast now." She pushes a button; the chandelier turns orange, and Davy Crockett appears standing inside the chapel of the Alamo. Chuck and Bob edge in to get a look. She looks at Mark. "He doesn't look like Fess Parker."

"Who?" asks Nate.

"Go meet your new friend, Mark."

Mark eases over in awe. "Colonel Crockett, please step down and come this way."

"I reckon I've done gone on to my reward. Are you one of those angels?"

"No sir, I'm Mark Right. This is not heaven. This is Lewisburg, Kentucky, and you are very much alive."

"Lewisburg, Kentucky. I've made it through there a time or two. I recollect there were a lot of hogs in the streets."

"That's not the problem today, but we do need your help. Oh, this is Miss February, as her sash says, Nate, Chuck and Bob."

"Pleased to meet you all. Young lady, you dress like a few Indian maidens I've seen."

"I'll take that as a compliment, sir."

Crockett spots the remains of the snake and the Pterodactyl. "We got some big critters in Tennessee, but I've never seen nothing like that."

"Colonel, you haven't seen anything yet. Please wait patiently, and hopefully, this will all make sense in a bit."

"I reckon it's better here than the spot I was in."

A few minutes later, Sergeant Alvin C. York steps out of the portal. "He doesn't look like Gary Cooper," February whispers to Mark.

"Who?" asks Nate.

Sergeant York is wearing his dress uniform, and the medal of honor hangs around his neck, having just been awarded to him, which was the date Mark remembered. He is as wide-eyed as the previous arrival and immediately recognizes his fellow Tennessean. "Davy Crockett. Praise God. I must be in heaven."

"Sergeant York, sir, I'm Mark Right. You are not in heaven. You are alive and in Lewisburg, Kentucky."

"Lewisburg, I hear they got a big stockyard there."

"They used to."

The Sergeant spies February in her skimpy outfit. "God bless you, young lady. You must hail from a very poor family to have to appear like that."

"February laughs. "I'm fine, sir. Don't worry about me, but it is an honor to meet you."

"Sergeant, why don't you step over and meet Davy Crockett," suggests Mark.

"This is a miracle the Lord has brought."

"It certainly is, and we're going to bring one more." He walks up to the control counter and looks at February with a somber glance. "General George S. Patton, early morning December 6, 1945." A button push later General Patton appears standing on stage with his wrecked car behind him.

"He doesn't look like George C. Scott," says February.

"Who?" says Nate.

"Go say hi, Mark," smiles February.

Mark is trembling. "Oh, boy. General Patton, sir, please step this way."

"I was in a gawd-damned wreck and ... (He spots Davy Crockett) ... I'll be damned! I've made it to heaven, sonuvabitch!"

"Sir, you are alive and in Lewisburg, Kentucky."

"Lewisburg? Sergeant York? Is this part of the army base?"

"No. The base is nearby, but we need your help here."

The general notices Miss February. "Young lady, I've seen a lot of camouflage in my time, but yours is most impressive."

"Thank you, general." She walks over to Mark, putting her hand on his shoulder. "Mr. Right, I think you need to make a speech. And it had better be damned good."

Mark realizes Davy Crockett, Sergeant York and General Patton are all staring at him. "Sure thing ... no pressure at all."

"Young man," prompts Patton. "I suggest you tell us what the hell is going on here."

"Gentlemen, this is an unusual moment in time. I'm not sure how it has happened, but in this large building, because of this machine (points to the portal) time has opened and brought us together. It has also brought evil here. General Patton, Stalin is here."

"Stalin! That sonuvabitch! Colonel Crockett, Sergeant York, Stalin is one bad guy."

"He has Trotsky and a murderous band of men with him. They have killed United States citizens. Also, three of our own people, including the man who owns this building, have gone over to his side. If they gain control of this place, they can control time. If they control time, they can erase democracy, real American democracy, from history. They must be stopped.

It is fate that you three men are here. We brought

you here, but, in a way, you were already selected. Colonel Crockett, your gun, Old Betsy, is here, and you will be reunited shortly."

"Praise the Lord. I sure have been missin' her."

"Sergeant York, your Army rifle from the Argonne is waiting for you."

"The Lord sure do work in mysterious ways."

"General Patton, your helmet, riding crop and field glasses are nearby."

Patton ponders for a moment. "This must be a miracle that God has brought upon us."

"Sir, it is a miracle. You three are great heroes from different times in a great American history. On this day in this spot, we are standing in the 21st century. But over a quarter of the way into this century, the United States of America is in trouble. Many of her own people have turned against her. Dangerous radicals have achieved power.

"How could this happen?" Patton is becoming outraged.

Mark continues. "They lied. They cheated. Then they lied about their cheating. They embraced foreign invaders. They devalued the honor of being a United States citizen. Because America is a nation of citizens.

"You're gawd-damned right it is," shouts Miss February in true Patton style. The general is impressed.

They are erasing freedom of speech and putting patriots in jail. If Stalin makes it out of this mall today, these people will embrace him as a comrade and throw in with him. Statues and monuments have already been destroyed, like the ones for the brave Christopher Columbus, who sailed off into the unknown and who I think I have seen here today, as he is no longer considered a hero. The once beautiful cities of this country are being turned into festering third-world hell-holes. General, you would be shocked at the condition of your hometown of Los Angeles."

"Sonuvabitch!"

"There is even a group of tyrants called extreme K.A.L.A. democrats. That stands for "Keep America Lousy Always," which is exactly what they intend to do."

"The bastards!"

"What we do here today, in this time, will help the United States retake its place in history as the best country that has ever existed or will ever exist. General Patton, Sergeant York, Colonel Crockett, will you lead this fight?"

Crockett leads off. "I reckon this here fight needs to be fought."

Sergeant York is reverent. "Lord be willing. I be with you."

General Patton is ready. "Let us work together and kill these Russian bastards."

Miss February kisses Mark. "Great speech. You

might have a future in politics."

"God, I hope not."

CHAPTER 14
Preparing to Kick Bolshevik Ass

In the manor house, J.P. Forte walks out of the business office and approaches Garmon, who is intensely staring at a bank of monitors. "Hey, your great dictator buddy took a shit in one of your cubicles back there. He says his new leaf girl is asleep so he wants you to bring him some oak leaves."

"Oh, good Lord."

"What the fuck are you looking at?"

"I'm trying to see what Mark Right is up to, but a lot of the monitoring system is out. Probably dinosaur damage. And why did they have to kill those noble creatures? They were worth a fortune alive."

"You got a fucking time thing going on here; you can get some more of the bastards."

"Maybe I will." Garmon taps on a monitor and, coincidentally, a picture appears. "Hey, there goes

Right. He's in one of my carts with ... General Patton?"

"Patton, that foul-mouthed son of a bitch? He was a motherfucker who cussed too goddamned much."

"We would not want anything like that around here." Garmon taps on some more monitors with no luck.

"I'm going out one of the tunnels to look for that bitch, Hotwad. I sent him to find my awards, but he's probably jerking off somewhere. And I think I saw Steve Love with some naked whore, so I'm going to try to get some footage."

"Be careful. Those crazy bitches on the west side have guns. They shot at a couple of Stalin's men who were on patrol. I wish I had put that gun store on this side of the mall. But Josef's men, with their own fine weapons, should rule the day."

"If by fine weapons, you mean a goddamned toilet filled with vodka, then yeah, because those bastards done set up another one over there at the OK Credit Union."

"Good God."

"And they started a bitch of a bonfire. They're burning bras and panties from Victoria's Secret, real fucking freaks. Hey, you got any vegetable soup around this pissed-up poor excuse for a mall?"

"I don't know. Go make yourself some T-Rex burgoo."

"Not a bad idea. Fuckalicious!"

"By the way, have you seen Nelson's bowler?"

"That bullshit sissy hat? It's back there in the office."

"Good old Nelson, always looking after the business."

"Uh, yeah, whatever. My ass is outta here."

Stalin has now crept up on Garmon. He carries the bowler, which has some ominous new stains on it. "Spoon face, you did not bring me oak leaves, so I had to use this." He tosses the hat on Garmon's console.

"You wiped your ass with Nelson's hat! That's from Savile Row!"

"It very soft. Help with damnable itching." He scratches his ass.

"Do you think your men could stop drinking vodka from a toilet and burning women's underwear long enough to help me conquer time?"

"We are ready. We will con time, and we will queer it."

"Close enough. I hope."

The cart bearing the heroes of the hour now pulls into the west wing with Miss February at the wheel. Davy Crockett was leery of the horseless conveyance at first but quickly embraced it as a new adventure from the strange time he found himself in. Mark left Chuck and Bob to guard the time portal and told Nate not to let anyone touch the control panel who was not wearing a camo bikini. During the one-mile trip, he tried to explain things to his new comrades. He talked about the dead dinosaurs they would see;

he tells them about Garmon Spooneybarger and tries to explain the calendar shoot in context of the women being scantily clad. Davy Crockett did have a little trouble grasping the concept of photography but is able to relate it to a painting. He tells General Patton that most of Stalin's men seem to be named Sergei. The general assures him they will die just as well under any name.

The crew climbs out of the cart, and introductions are made. Everyone except June is impressed by Sergeant York's Medal of Honor. General Patton is captivated by the well-armed Calendar cadre. He is delighted to find that Miss July is a member of the Army reserve and offers compliments on her "uniform of the day." He promotes her to sergeant and confers the title of honorary private on the non-military people present. This excites Mark who always regretted not serving. Miss June dismisses it, claiming that her private parts are not honorary.

Upon his first look at the dead dinosaurs, Davy Crockett has one thought. "These big varmints are about as ugly as old Mike Fink and smell just as bad."

"From what I've read about your rival, Mr. Fink, they are also as mean as he was," adds Mark.

After taking a moment to salute the dead, except the dead Bolsheviks, and visiting with the wounded, General Patton leads Crockett and York into the gun store. He inspects their artifact weapons and deems them fit for combat then claims his own items. Crockett and York are happy to see their old friends.

"Betsy, I sure missed you. I should have taken you to that Alamo. It was a tough situation there."

Sergeant York looks at his rifle. "I used you once when I had to, and it looks like I have to again."

There are black powder supplies in the store and plenty of cartridges for York's rifle, so soon the pair is ready to go and step out for a little target practice.

Mark tells Patton that his friend had spotted Stalin going in the manor house and some of the Bolshevik soldiers in front of the OK Credit Union just down the east wing.

"And where is this friend of yours now, Private Right."

Mark takes out his radio. "I'll try to raise him, sir. Steve … Come in Steve … Steve? He's not answering."

"Does he, by any chance, have a horse?" The general points his riding crop at a horse standing on the edge of the sub-atrium; its reins are tied to the safety rail.

"No, but I know who does."

A few minutes later, Steve Love walks up the steps and into the atrium. He is fastening his belt with his right hand and carrying his shirt in his left. The cross around his neck is swinging back and forth. Seeing Mark waiting for him, he is excited to share some news. "Dude! I just banged Lady Godiva! And

I flushed Trotsky down the sewer."

"That's great, Steve. Meet General George S. Patton, Jr."

"Holy fuck!" He pulls on his shirt and throws up a salute."

"Nice shirt, Private Love; what were you doing down there?"

"Private?"

"We're in the Army now," smiles Mark.

"Cool beans." Steve is pleased as he also wishes he had served.

Lady Godiva walks up behind Steve, touching his butt. "Passion. Passion."

"She doesn't talk much," states Steve. "Uh, General Patton, this is Lady Godiva."

"Madame." He taps his riding crop on his helmet and then looks at Steve. "I see this is more history stuff. You look like a sonuvabitch who could handle this situation."

"Thank you, sir."

"I am curious to learn if you might be able to step away from this naked lady long enough to help us fight some gawddamned Russians."

"Yes, sir!" Steve helps Lady Godiva on her horse, unties the reins and leads her back to the area around the gun store that Patton has established as the rear echelon. The women (except one) are friendly to her. Aria Stanzer is impressed by the horse. Steve figures she can help in the hospital. June feels it necessary to get off a catty remark.

"Like, why don't you put on some clothes, bitch?"

This attracts a sharp dagger from September. "You're not exactly wearing a ball gown, you stupid twit."

"Don't call my tit stupid. Both my beauties are as smart as yours."

"It would take two of yours to be as smart as one of mine."

"I'm glad I'm not burdened with much of those things," says March.

"You make up for it in other places," gigs December, touching her own butt.

"You don't know what you're missing, girl," smiles August as she squeezes her pair."

"Enough of this!" yells Patton. "We've got work to do."

One hour of intense training is launched. First: the fitness center. Steve, Mark, February, and July run on treadmills as the General "encourages" them. August then takes a turn as Patton "encourages" her, and Mark and Steve drool.

About halfway down the west wing, Davy Crockett and Sergeant York decide to use the two dead T-Rexes for target practice. They are about 200 yards from one and 220 yards from the other. York admires Crockett's weapon. "Old Betsy looks like a fine gun, Colonel. How fast can you reload her?"

"I figure if I'm at my best, about six seconds."

"Impressive."

After a couple of shots each to find their range, the pair quickly removes the three remaining ears from the two targets and then alternate on the eyeballs. Pop! Pop! Pop! Pop! Suddenly, a weird man, not previously seen, appears out of nowhere. "Alvin York done cut dead dinosaur five times!"

"I reckon that guy is a might irritatin'," states York.

"I reckon so," concurs Crockett.

Outside the mall, at the main entrance, Burley Dick approaches a SWAT officer.

"I.M.G.I.N.! I must get inside now!"

"No one is going inside this mall, sir."

"By whose authority?"

"Mine. I'm in charge here." He points to the captain's bars on his collar.

"I'm a production manager. I'm the only true authority here."

"Sir, are you drunk?"

"I don't drink. That's medication."

Suddenly, the strange man appears beside Burley Dick. "Burley Dick done cut AA meetin's five times."

Back inside, General Patton gives instruction in basic arms, hand-to hand-combat and hand grenades. Lumina Salazar serves a quick snack, and everyone is "encouraged" to eat. Even June consumes an extra olive. Mark and Steve ask for a quick restroom run, and the General goes along to "encourage" them.

Now, a plan is laid out. General Patton has determined that the four dead T-Rexes scattered around the atrium will make excellent defensive positions. The first two carcasses, about 20 feet away from the west wing with a narrow gap between them, is where the rear guard will be tasked with protecting the gun store and the hospital. This is made up of January, March, April, May, August, November, and December. June is "encouraged" to help in the hospital with Lady Godiva or just stay out of the way.

The third Rex (the bikini-top pervert) is on its back, dead-center in the atrium. September, with her Winchester, and February, with Mr. Mossberg, will be stationed here to watch the flanks. The fourth pile of future fossil fuel lays only about 30 feet from the manor house with his back to the building. The front line, made up of General Patton, Sergeant York, Davy Crockett, Miss July (the now Sergeant Striker), Mark and Steve, will start at this point.

The preparations are made; only one more thing is needed. "Sergeant York," requests General Patton. "Will you lead us in a prayer?"

"My honor, sir." Everyone takes a knee except June, who sits on her skinny butt.

Sergeant York bows his head. "Dear Lord, this is a most unusual day that you have made for us. I don't rightly understand it all, but it seems that we must fight. You helped me fight once before, and I respectfully ask that you help me again and help my new friends and comrades. Please guide us to victory today so that you may create a new day tomorrow that be free from conflict. In Jesus's name, I pray. Amen."

Everyone repeats "Amen," even June.

It is time to fight.

CHAPTER 15
The Battle of the Taj Ma-Mall or Saving Time

The good guys are in position. There is no sign of the enemy at the manor house or the OK Credit Union which sits 20 yards away and catty-cornered from the house. Abruptly, the metal plate over the manor house door slides open followed by the actual door. Stalin emerges flanked by Miss October on his left and Garmon Spooneybarger on his right. "Please come forward," urges Garmon. "My friend Josef wants to talk."

General Patton steps from behind the dinosaur, warns York, Crockett and July to watch for snipers, and he motions to Mark and Steve to move forward with him. Steve walks on his right, Mark on his left. Mark figures that being just to the left of General Patton is still pretty far right. They proceed until the two trios are ten feet apart. Stalin recognizes Patton from a picture he saw in the book on soviet history. "You general I see in book. You give small help to Soviet Union when they win the great war."

"That was a gawd-damned mistake."

"Then it is not a goddamned mistake to kill you. My friend, Spoonbread, see other phony American heroes on his box of magic. He say Davy Crockett and Sergeant Alvin York also be here."

"We have adequate personnel to defeat you."

"But we offer deal. Surrender now, and we give you dignified execution."

"What kind of a deal is that you sonuvabitch?"

"It good deal. You surrender or die like dogs on field of confliction fighting beside almost naked women."

"We don't feel like dying today. It's you bastards who are going to die."

Quickly the metal plate over a dormer window slides open and a Sergei bursts through the glass, pointing his rifle at the General. Simultaneously, Crockett, York and July fire into him and he drops out to the ground. Garmon runs back inside.

"You just lost a Sergei," shouts Mark. "And Spooneybarger ran away."

"I no need Spoonhead to kill you, and I have plenty Sergeis, and strong Russian women always obedient to make more."

"I'll help you make more Sergeis," crows Miss October.

"You are not sturdy for Sergeis; maybe you make another Trotsky."

"Joey, you're bad!"

"Having boyfriend trouble, October bitch?" needles Steve.

"No! He loves me."

"I've heard that one before."

"Time to kill," yells Stalin. "Sergei!" Fourteen Sergeis run out of the OK Credit Union and line up shoulder-to-shoulder with their rifles pointed.

Patton motions September forward to get behind the first dead Rex with his other rifles. February will lay back waiting for closer action. Now he is lined up with Mark and Steve, facing the Sergeis with four guns backing them up. The enemy starts to advance with a chant. "Fuck General Patton! Fuck Sergeant York! Fuck Davy Crockett! Kill them all! Da! Da! Da!"

Crockett looks at York. "These fellers are not very polite."

"They are not, Colonel."

Garmon runs out of the house with his bowler on. "Dear chaps. We must not fight. We can work something out."

"What's on his hat?" Steve asks Mark.

"It looks like shit."

"Is this guy nuts?" questions Patton.

"Yes, sir he is," answers Mark.

Stalin is confused. "Gar-spoon, what the hell?

Now you English guy. You one guy who act like two? You are stranger than Trotsky."

Nelson bloviates on in his Nelson persona. "We can reach a deal here. If you Yanks surrender, perhaps Josef will give you a mild prison sentence of ten years."

"Da, I give ten years and work you to death in two."

J.P. Forte and Hotwad enter the atrium from the south as the battle is about to break out. "Fuck! yells Forte, as he puts his camera on his shoulder. I got me some bitching video to shoot. Hotwad, you ass licking freak. Find my knob and get to polishing."

Hotwad stares at the dead T-Rex laying on its back. "I'll climb up here and look around for Mr. Forte's knob."

Garmon steps in front of Stalin, with his back to the combatants. "Please do not shoot my dear friend, Mr. Stalin."

"Then, I'll shoot your ass!" yells Mark as he fires a round into Nelson's rump.

"God save the King!" screams Nelson running into the house with the door and metal plate closing behind him, leaving Stalin and October trapped outside and enraged.

"Damn you, Spoonface! You English cake fruit! You ferryboat captain!"

The enemy advances. Patton orders his rifles to fire as he, Mark, and Steve hustle out of the way.

Crockett, York, July and September discharge, each taking down a Sergei. The remaining Sergeis fire, and Crockett's cap is shot off as he reloads. York's Medal of Honor deflects a bullet meant for him. The quartet fires again, and two more Bolsheviks are erased. Four Sergeis scream, "Sergei is dead!" and retreat to the safety of the credit union. Four Bolsheviks remain. One is able to dodge bullets and disappear around the left flank. One attempts to lead Stalin and October to safety behind the elevator shaft. The other two charge Mark and Steve, who are prepared with a mental inventory of moves gleaned from years of watching classic action movies and TV shows. The four fight hand-to-hand.

Mark punches and yells, "Kiss my ass you bastard!"

Steve wails away, "We're going to be roommates in hell!"

"Fuck me, Batman!" Yells Forte as he records the action.

The attackers of Mark and Steve quickly get enough and run away toward the west and south. One catches a bullet in his shoulder from Sergeant York's rifle.

"Go after Stalin," barks General Patton.

Miss February runs after Stalin and October with Mark and Steve following. The Sergei with them is slowed after Steve puts a round in his leg, allowing February to finish him off with the Mossberg. She racks and sets her sights on blowing the smirk off October's face but steps on a glob of grease that earlier fell off Hotwad's hair and goes down dropping her gun. October runs on. Stalin grabs February by the arm, pulls her to her feet, places his cocked pistol to her head and moves toward the elevator. "Let go of me, you smelly bastard. Do you ever brush your teeth?" shouts February.

"Stay calm," yells Mark.

"Now you all stop the shoot," orders Stalin. "Or this bitch not live to pull plow."

"I'll pull you straight to hell," bellows February.

Stalin now has her in front of the elevator. "Before Spoon go nutable, he tell me about button that go up." He pushes the button, the door opens, and he forces February in. "We go up now. She come down soon." The door closes. The elevator creeps upward.

General Patton is concerned. "The bastard's going to throw her over the side."

Mark motions Steve toward the jetpack display. "I've got an idea, General."

"Dude!" Steve squeals.

The jetpack is secured to the floor by a chain locked to an eyebolt. Mark shoots the chain in two and pulls it off. Steve helps him strap on the device. "Roadie, can you fly this thing?"

"I watched a YouTube video on it just the other day."

"I thought you only had dialup at home?"

"I watched it at work on Burley's time." Mark tightly grips the handles and tries to manage his shaking. "Let's see. Thrust on the right. Direction on the left. And the video suggested insulated pants for this, but I don't have time to worry about that. So, Steve, you got any Beeman's?"

Steve smiles. "I might have me a stick."

"Then loan me some. I'll pay you back later."

"Fair enough."

On the observation deck, the elevator door opens and Stalin shoves February out but is overcome by the urge to scratch his ass, giving her time to smack the gun away and grab his arm spinning them around and around as they move toward the sub-standard safety rail. The rail stops their whirling as she pushes him over, but it breaks loose, and she falls too.

Mark shouts "Fuck!" and launches skyward. As the sensation of a quick ascent moves through him an even louder "Fuck!" is uttered. Stalin and the railing are dodged, and February falls between his arms grabbing on tight. "Hi, I've been meaning to catch you before you got away."

"I was almost out of here," she smiles.

Having been oblivious to the fighting, and still standing on the T-Rex, Hotwad looks up and sees something falling toward him. "That's funny. Something is falling toward me." Stalin slams, backside first, into Hotwad's head, piledriving him deep in the carcass. His fall broken, Stalin rolls, picks up his hat that had fallen off, and runs away as the railing bounces off Hotwad's exposed head that is sticking out of the dinosaur. "Whoa, I think I have a skull fracture."

Forte gets a closeup of his assistant. "Smile Hotbitch! I didn't know you were into dinosaurs."

Mark and February land to the applause of their comrades. Steve helps him off with the pack. "Marcus that was the greatest thing I've ever seen, and I've seen a hell of a lot today."

Patton shakes his hand. "Soldier, you're going to get a commendation for this."

"Thank you, sir."

February prepares to plant one on him. "And you're going to get a very wet kiss."

"Thank you, ma'am."

Crockett picks up his cap, amazed at what he has seen. York says a prayer of thanks.

Forte charges in with his camera. "That was fuckin' great, other guy. It was better than East Lick-a-Dick, Assachusetts."

Patton smacks Forte in the face with his riding crop. "Gawd-damn it. No shaggy haired civilian sonuvabitch will utter obscenities in the presence of a general officer of the United States Army!"

"Whoa. Brass-cock."

An urgent call comes thru Mark's radio, and he informs Patton: "General, they're under attack at the time portal and running low on bullets."

"Private Love, get down there with York and Crockett. Take the cart and take them some ammo!"

"Yes, sir."

"Sergeant Striker and Private September. Advance behind the manor house onto the golf course, and keep an eye on that credit union. Right and February, sweep the area for Stalin and the ones who got through."

Everyone scrambles to fulfill their new orders, as Forte rubs his face and Hotwad remains inside the dinosaur.

The flanking Sergei has cut between two dinosaur bodies and snuck up on the rear guard. Not wanting to waste bullets on weak American women, he draws his knife, creeps up behind December and slices off a piece of her right butt cheek that protrudes from her bathing suit. Her scream alerts the others, and they spring into action. March hits him in the face with mace. January cracks his kneecap with a kick, but he penetrates her thigh with his blade. August discharges her derringer into his chest and shouts a war cry, "44 double D or fight!"

The attacker is slowing down as April slices off his left thumb with the bowie knife and November smashes his nose with her spatula. May slaps him with her whip then blows a hole in his carcass with her magnum. Godiva's horse kicks him in the head as he goes down. Lady Godiva accesses the situation and tears a couple of strips off her silk blanket to help the wounded. June accuses them of being murderers. May asks Lady G for an extra strip to gag June with.

Mark spots a blood trail leading into the heavy brush along Catgrass Creek. He approaches cautiously, but wounded shoulder Sergei zips out of the brush and puts his ready pistol against Mark's forehead as Mark greets him. "Well, hello commie bastard."

"Stupid American, you will not flatulate me with your flaccid humor. I kill you now." A shotgun blast rings out, and the Sergei's right arm disappears in a bloody mist from mid-bicep to the wrist. The hand and gun fall to the ground, squeezing off a shot into the ceiling along the way. The Sergei screams and pulls a knife from his belt, but another blast rings out and his left arm disappears in the same manner, the hand and knife dropping.

Gaining the upper hand, Mark punches his would-be killer in the face and sends him falling into Catgrass Creek to bleed out. February struts up with the Mossberg smoking, and racks it, a spent shell flying out. "I shot and disarmed a man."

"He should have kept his arms if he wanted to fight with your friend," Mark replies, wiping the blood spatter off his face. He gets excited as February reloads with the five shells from her bikini bottom. They are about to kiss when a bullet whizzes past their heads. A Sergei and October are spotted standing in the creek 30 feet ahead. Mark returns fire. The Sergei streaks up the east bank and into a Subway Sandwich shop. October flashes up the west bank, her red bikini butt driving the engine. Her four-inch Christian Louboutin's pumping away.

"You get the creep; I'll get the bitch," shouts February. When they vacate the area, Leonardo Da Vinci steps out of the brush with his sketch pad under his arm, picks up the spent shell and places it in his pocket.

Mark swiftly gets to the Subway and sees that the Sergei's attention has been grabbed by a three-foot sub, a special promotional item being tested at the Taj Ma-Mall. As the hungry thug prepares to take a bite, Mark picks up another three-footer and challenges him. In a flash, the two face off and are flailing the sandwiches at each other. The combatants are soon peppered with severe mustard and mayonnaise stains about the head and shoulders and nicks from sharp banana peppers.

Mark feels a one liner is called for. "For a loser from a bread-challenged country, you handle a loaf well."

"Fuck your American bread, and perhaps stick it up your ass." As this is the broken-hand Sergei, he loses his grip on the sandwich. It falls to the floor, so he draws his pistol in pain, forgetting something important. He pulls the trigger and ... nothing.

Mark tosses his own sub at his forgetful opponent and draws the 1911. "You've got to cock that one. Not this one." Two shots into the heart ends the affair, and Mark looks down at the fallen. "You disappoint me, young Bolshevik."

General Patton enters the Subway. "Good work, private. The rear guard told me they got one, and there's a dead one in the creek."

"The work of Miss February, sir. She's hunting for red October butt right now."

"She can handle that. Let's get back to the credit union and clean up there. Keep an eye out for Stalin."

Two hundred and ten yards out from the time portal, Steve spots Chuck and Bob standing on the west bank near the footbridge and stops the cart. "What happened, guys?"

Bob tries to explain." They came in through the hole in the wall, got behind us and flushed us out. Nate was supposed to watch that spot, but he was fascinated with that damned dead snake and didn't see them. Now, he's their prisoner."

Chuck adds more. "There's four of them. One is acting like a sergeant."

"That's Ivan," says Steve as he hands them a box of ammo then turns around and folds down the rear facing third seat of the cart to create a flat surface. "Let's haul some appliances down there as close as we can and build a barricade. Then we'll figure out the rest."

Miss February sees a red flash run into an ice cream shoppe called Frozen Assets. She enters and finds her quarry staring back at her. The shop has an old-fashioned soda fountain and a floor-to-ceiling freezer case with pints and quarts that are starting to melt because the power is out in this part of the mall.

"Your mass-murderer boyfriend tried to kill me, bitch."

"I guess I'll have to finish the job for him, you camo skank."

February sets down her shotgun and removes her sash. October tosses her sash to the ground, and they gravitate toward each other. At three feet apart, they slap each other in the face. At two feet, they rip each other's bikini tops off. At one foot, they kiss passionately until February pushes October away. "You taste like a commie-whore."

October punches February hard in the face and slides over the counter. "Come and get me."

February follows. They grab each other by the throat and thrash around smashing the glass out of the freezer case while suffering cuts on their shoulders and breasts in the process. February pops the lid off a pint of vanilla and dumps it on October's breasts.

"You just got creamed on, slut."

October bounces a quart of raspberry off February's face. "I'll berry your flabby ass." Then she pulls the camo bikini bottom open and pours in orange sherbet. "Chill out, you nasty bitch."

February ponders the feeling for a moment then smashes a pint of cherry in October's face. "It's been a long time since your cherry was popped." Gaining the upper hand, February forces October under a spigot and unleashes chocolate syrup over her face and breasts. "Once you've had black, you'll never go back."

October pulls away and slips over the counter picking up her sash in the process. When February follows, she gets the sash snapped in her face, stunning her and allowing her adversary to wrap the satin strip around February's neck, dragging her to the ground as she pulls it tight. "When you fade to black, you ain't coming back, you crazy cunt."

February can't breathe and needs to think fast. With her right hand she unzips her left boot, slides it off and grips it by the cuff. Quickly, she snaps the boot over her head, contacting October's face and feeling the sash loosen. Two more hits and the grip is broken. February struggles to her feet gasping for air and pounds October's face with the boot three more times, dropping the commie lover on her back unconscious, the red soles of her Louboutin's exposed.

February staggers to the counter and grabs a napkin, wipes the chocolate, blood and tissue from her boot heel then puts the it back on. She looks at October's face. "You should put something cold on that before it swells." Retrieving a slushy pint of Neapolitan, she pours it on the bloody face. "That should do it." Still gasping, she picks up October's top and tosses it near her. "If you come around, do the world a favor and cover up those dog-eared tits." Feeling the nakedness of her own mammary area, she picks up her top and fastens it on. Finally catching her breath, she kneels beside October, scrapes chocolate off her enemy's right breast with her right middle finger and puts it in her mouth. "Mmm, I love chocolate."

Several feet away stands J.P. Forte who has taped the whole fight. "Boob-o-rama, I've got to find a quiet corner and handle this situation."

Across from the OK Credit Union, July and September are crouched in a sand trap when they are joined by General Patton and Mark. "Report, Sergeant," orders Patton.

"One of the enemy emerges now and then to stoke the fire, sir."

"What's in that toilet?" wonders Patton.

"Vodka, sir," replies Mark. "They drink out of it."

"Good Lord, they're gawd-damned third world."

After a few minutes, the door opens, and a Sergei

walks out with a mug that says, "I just work here for the free paper clips and rubber bands."

As the thirsty man approaches the toilet, General Patton hands Mark a hand grenade. "He's going to need a chaser. Can you, do it?"

"I'll make it." Mark pulls the pin and lobs the grenade, knowing it doesn't have to be close but thinking it would be nice if it landed in the center of the bowl with a "kerplunk," which is what it does. The ensuing explosion showers the Sergei with porcelain bits and vodka. He falls on the smoldering fire, the vodka on him reigniting the flames.

"Great toss, private."

"Thank you, sir. I love the smell of burning vodka in the morning. It smells like victory."

Another Sergei looks out and slams the door shut as July and September fire on him. General Patton scans the area with his field glasses and spots something. "There's a bulldozer about half a klick east of here. Cover me." Patton works his way down the golf course, angles across the promenade and approaches the machine. It is an older Caterpillar with no computerized enhancements, so the General effects a quick hotwire, and the yellow beast roars to life with a powerful growl.

A few minutes later, General Patton lines the Cat up to face the OK Credit Union, raising the blade halfway. "Fall in behind me, we're going in." The façade is quickly breeched. Patton jumps off, drawing his Smith and Wesson. July, September, and Mark fan out behind him. They search the building, but there are no Bolsheviks to be found. Sergeant Striker looks in a broom closet and finds an open escape hatch in the floor. "Over here, General."

"Sonuvabitch! Too dangerous to go in there after them. They have to come out somewhere. Stand back." He pulls a grenade from his pocket, pulls the pin and drops it in the hole as he kicks the hatch shut. Everyone feels a rumble under their feet. "Private Right. Check in with the other front."

"Yes, sir, but I must say you drive a mean bulldozer."

"Not that much different than a tank, private."

On the south end, Steve, Davy Crockett, Sergeant York, Chuck and Bob have fetched and wrestled a chest freezer, a dishwasher and a dryer into position on the east bank 57 feet from the photo store and are crouched behind the barricade. The maneuver had some difficulty, with the cart only able to operate on the west promenade because of the security wall blocking the east side. They had to haul the appliances to near the end of the westside run, and then carry them across the creek while using the footbridge as cover from Bolshevik potshots.

Mark raises Steve on the walkie, and the situation is relayed. Mark then requests that the cart be sent for General Patton. "Bob and Chuck," requests Steve.

"Go pick up the General at the credit union." The twosome splash across the creek to the cart and are gone.

Steve can see Ivan and the three Sergeis milling around inside the photo store giving Nate a hard time. Then he has an idea. "Sergeant York, this might be a good time for your turkey call."

"How do you know about that?"

"It was in the movie. Oh, I guess you haven't seen that yet."

"One of them moving pictures. About me?"

"Yes sir. It was a good one."

"They ain't got no sound. How did people hear the call?"

"By the time your movie comes out, there's going to be sound. Trust me."

"I reckon we can give it a shot." He puts his right hand to his mouth. "Gobble! Gobble! Gobble!" A Sergei sticks his head out of the doorway, and Crockett drops him.

"Cool!" shouts Steve. He takes out his 1911 and stretches his arms across the freezer top. "Let go another one."

Gobble! Gobble! Gobble!"

Another Sergei sticks his head out, and Steve cancels him. "This is great!" York attempts a couple more calls, but Ivan and the other Sergei are not biting.

"You know fellers," speaks Crockett. "I was once in a spot like this and had some success with a Shawnee war cry." York and Steve nod in affirmation. "As I recall, it went something like this: "EEEEEEEEEEEEEEEEAAAAAAAAAAAAAHHHHHHHHHHHHAAAAAAAAAAA!!!!!!!!!!!!!!!!!!" A wide-eyed Sergei appears in the doorway, and Steve and the Sergeant team up to shatter his breastbone.

"Woo-hoo!" shouts Steve. "Hey Ivan! You want to surrender?"

Ivan shouts out. "I no surrender up. I kill you all. Then I find Spock and kill him."

"Who is this Spock feller?" wonders Sergeant York.

"Spock's not here. That guy is just nuts." Before they can deal with Ivan the trio hears a commotion approaching from behind and turn to find a flying wedge of five Bolsheviks surrounding Stalin, Miss October and J.P. Forte running toward them. The still woozy and chocolatey October who did manage to redon her top, is being dragged along by Stalin, the yellow Louboutin's barely hanging on by the straps. Forte carries his Golden Knob award in his left hand, his video camera in his right and his equipment bag over his shoulder. The attackers break out in a chant. "Here comes the mighty ass. We will kill you all so he may pass." They fire their rifles at the trio. Crockett and York return fire, taking out a Sergei on each flank. The remaining group veers into the creek to avoid the barricade. Crockett, Steve and York jump into the stream to face them.

One Sergei charges Crockett who grabs him by the shoulder and hip and tosses him thru the air. Sergeant York grabs the rifle from his attacker and smashes him in the face with his own butt. During this action, Stalin, October and Forte try to slip by. Steve trips Forte then feels a punch on the back of his neck and spins around to find a Sergei with a pistol pointed at him, so he has to think quickly. "Dude! Let's play Russian roulette! You go first."

"Da. Americans always lose Russian roulette." The Sergei puts his pistol to his head and blows his brains out."

"Not this time, dumbass." Steve turns to the prone Forte. "I'm going to kick your ass."

"Bitchery. Dickery. Cock, Love. I'm not a fighter."

"With biceps like that, you should use them."

He makes a shaking motion with his hand. "I do use the bastards." He jumps up, grabs his camera and runs away leaving the knob behind.

Stalin, October, Forte and the two Sergeis roughed up by Crockett and York make it into the photo store, climbing over the dead bodies at the entrance. Steve, Crockett and York reassemble behind the barricade. The cart pulls up on the other side of the creek, and Patton splashes across Catgrass Creek followed by Mark, February, Chuck, and Bob, who has a slight shoulder wound after being grazed by a Sergei's bullet on the way out. Patton has left Sergeant Striker and

September at Bolshevicky to secure it in case any enemy return there.

Mark and Steve smile at each other like two possums sneaking into a persimmon festival. "Having fun, Steve?"

"You know it, Marcus. General Patton, sir, I must report that Stalin is inside there with three men, his girlfriend, that camera guy you smacked and a prisoner named Nate who can run the time equipment."

The general is concerned. "If Stalin can force that guy to control time, he may bring 10,000 men here at any moment."

Mark and Miss February hug. "Miss February, you smell like orange sherbet. That was my favorite when I was a kid."

"It just might become your favorite again."

For Stalin's sake, he should have thought of the 10,000 men. But he chose another play that seemed like a good idea and calls out. "Hey general, I have present for you and your co-whores." The dictator appears in the entryway with Nate in front him and a pistol, borrowed from Ivan, pointed at the technician's head.

"Hold your fire for the moment," instructs Patton.

Ivan kicks the bodies out of the way, and the last two Sergeis walk out carrying a crude, roundish, metal, 19th century looking device that is ticking away.

"Looks like something from the *Wild, Wild West*,"

says Mark.

"I hope you mean the tv show and not that movie," returns Steve.

"You got it."

Stalin explains the setup. "My friend here help me obtain gift for you from wonderful maker of bombs, the great patriot, Nikolai Kibalchich, who blew up that smellable hog Alexander the number two. Very smart man, only problem he look like Trotsky. His bomb blow legs off stupid Tsar. It hilarious. Happen when I just a boy, but father always tell it to me as sleepy time story after nightly beating. Da, good times. Enjoy your big boom, Yankee dogs. When you dead I will wear York's shiny medal."

General Patton assesses the situation, pulls his Smith and Wesson and fires one shot into the bomb. It detonates, blowing the two bearers to bits. "Those are weak bombs and have a very small range," Patton explains. "And that sonuvabitch is not going to wear a Medal of Honor."

Steve wipes something off his cheek. "Damn! It's raining Sergeis."

"Another thing for the climate bozos to complain about," adds Mark.

"Fuck!" shouts Stalin. "Time to get Georgia on mind."

"Let's get in there, and finish it," orders Patton. Steve picks up the Bronze Knob, and the group enters the room to find Stalin, October and J.P. Forte on the stage surrounded by the Georgian countryside. Stalin still holds Ivan's pistol in his right hand. Nate is behind the console with Ivan holding a knife on him.

"Sergeant Ivan!" shouts Stalin. "Kill the general!"

"You have my gun, mighty ass."

"Use the knife, you damnable idiot."

Ivan growls and runs at Patton who swiftly shoots him dead. Forte jumps off the stage. "Forget this shit, I'm out."

Steve runs up to Forte. "No, you're in. And so is this." He pulls the back of Forte's jeans down, inserts the Bronze Knob and tosses him back on the stage.

"Fuck me," groans J.P. "I've been 'Loved' too much."

Stalin peels some dried chocolate off October's face and eats it. "Chocolate cow taste pretty good."

October screams at February, "I'll get you bitch!"

"Any time, any time period, you commie-loving trollop."

Stalin glares at Patton. I learn one good thing from west. He raises his left hand and extends the middle finger. "This for you, General." He also attempts to tip his hat with the other hand while still holding the gun.

Patton promptly shoots off the raised finger. "Fuck!" screams Stalin. His reaction to the shot causes him to fling his hat across the room and discharge his pistol into Nate who falls on the control panel, starting the ten-second countdown.

Suddenly, Trotsky dashes through the room carrying a book on USSR history and wearing a Houston Oilers football helmet. "Excuse me. Excuse me." He jumps on the stage. Patton fires a shot into Stalin's left shoulder as the image disappears.

The Battle of the Taj Ma-Mall is over.

CHAPTER 16
Mopping up and Getting a Little Pussy

Initially, General Patton was disappointed that Stalin had escaped but soon realized that his team had ruled the day and scored a great victory. Besides, Stalin was missing a finger and had a bullet in his shoulder. George couldn't praise the efforts of his makeshift team enough and wished he had a pocket of medals to hand out.

Mark was astounded at the events of the day and realized that he now had a great screenplay to write. Steve was glad J.P. Forte was gone and had a bronze knob up his ass. He was now thinking about his future and realized it might be in the past. Hotwad was still stuck in the remains of the T-Rex, and nobody cared.

The wounded Nate was loaded on the cart and transported by Chuck and Bob to the front entrance, in anticipation of first responders entering the mall.

Bob's own injury was minor and not bothering him. Miss February stepped behind the control panel to study how to send people home. She was soon able to inform Mark that people needed to be sent back within a minute of where they were picked up. This would make things tricky for Davy Crockett and the crewman from the *Titanic*.

The team, minus February, met halfway down the south wing, and a search was planned to look for Leonardo Da Vinci, Christopher Columbus, the guy from the *Titanic* and the lefthander from Brooklyn. Steve said he would take care of Lady Godiva.

Mark soon located number 19 and walked him over to a CVS drugstore to show him some modern arthritis treatments that he could take back. A bag was filled, and the pair set out for the time portal. On the way, Mark noticed an arrangement from Dick's, as even though their store was not yet open, they had a few items on display. One was a high-tech life vest for boaters. Mark brought it along.

Upon entering the photo store, Mark gets some news from Miss February.

"I know this is hard to believe, but September and June teamed up and brought in Columbus.

"Really?"

"The guy was very quiet. September said he was agitated when they first tried to bring him, so she delivered a smack upside the head to calm him down."

"And you sent him back?"

"To the deck of the Santa Maria."

"Are you sure it was him?"

"He smelled like he had been on a long sea voyage. Something wrong?"

"Naw. I'm sure it was fine. Get Ebbets Field on the line."

The historic ballpark appears, and a new friend goes home with some help for a problem that is destined to plague him. As Brooklyn disappears, Patton, York and Crockett enter with Leonardo Da Vinci. The general carries a bag from a liquor store. The Master carries a full sketch pad and a Subway bag with a foot long that he had constructed himself. General Patton can speak Italian, and the quartet seems to be enjoying each other's company. When Leonardo sees Miss February, he cuts loose with a big smile.

Just over a minute later, Leonardo is home. "What kind of sandwich do you think he had?" February asks Mark. "A meatball marinara seems right."

"Maybe or it could be, 'Da Vinci Code' cuts."

General Patton has scavenged a bottle of Pappy Van Winkle bourbon and some shot glasses. He invites Crockett and York into the back room to share a drink between military men and discuss their adventures before they part ways. Sergeant York will only take a very small drink, not wanting to rile up an old habit. Mark shows February the life vest and asks her to call up the *Titanic*. The deck of the mighty ship soon appears, and they stare in awe for a moment. Then Mark steps to the doorway and shouts "Iceberg! Iceberg dead ahead!"

A faint echo replies, "Iceberg! Iceberg!"

"Down here!" shouts Mark. The sound of approaching footsteps is picked up. They grow louder and louder and then the lookout is in the room. Mark tosses him the life vest and points to the stage. The man jumps on the deck and is gone in ten seconds.

"Should we have done something to save the ship," wonders February.

"Maybe that guy will do it this time." Mark raises Chuck on the radio and asks that a couple of special item be brought down.

Patton, York and Crockett reenter, and the General pours a shot for Mark and February. Sergeant York's medal of honor ceremony is recalled; the Sergeant requests that his gun be put back in the display case, and then he receives salutes from Patton and Crockett and makes a parting comment. "It was an honor to meet you all. And, boy, this was a heck of a day that the Lord made." Then he rejoins a day that the Lord made long ago.

Mark explains to Patton that Crockett's situation is a bit delicate, so the General should go next. When his just wrecked car appears, the steam rising form the ruptured radiator, he salutes Davy Crockett then turns and salutes Mark and February. "I had a helluva time here. I wish Ike had let me kill Russian bastards like you guys did."

Mark and February salute and respond in unison. "Our pleasure, sir. God bless you."

The General takes off his helmet, deposits his riding crop and field glasses into it, then sets it on the counter. "These should already be in the supply jeep." He enters the scene of the just happened wreck, opens his door and shouts to his aid, "Hap! I'm out here!" Then he returns to history. But what kind of history will it now be?

The cart pulls up, and Chuck scurries in carrying the Bell jetpack and a Houston Oilers helmet. "I fueled it up like you said, Mark."

Mark explains to Davy Crockett: "Colonel, we must send you back to a tricky situation. But if you could get out of there, you could keep on fighting. There's a big battle coming up after the Alamo at San Jacinto, and on that glorious day Texas will become free."

"That's the contraption that shot you in the air like a bird."

"I think it can help you, if you're willing."

"I sure would like to keep on fightin'."

Chuck and Mark strap the pack on Davy and a flight tutorial begins. After a few minutes, Crocket is ready to fly. He decides to take Old Betsy to the

Alamo with him this time. Mark hands him the football helmet. "You'll need this to crash through the roof."

Davy slides his new metal hat over his old coonskin one. "I reckon I had quite a time going to battle with you fine people."

"We enjoyed having you," says Mark. Miss February pushes a button, the interior of the Alamo chapel appears, and Colonel Davy Crockett returns to the battle.

"He was a nice guy," smiles February.

"Fess Parker would have been proud," muses Mark.

Steve Love enters wearing a white CVS pharmacy coat. With his left hand, he pushes a shopping cart crammed with Twinkies, over-the-counter pharmaceuticals, and a few things from behind the counter. His right hand leads Lady Godiva's horse with his new love aboard. "Hiiiii!!!!" Steve smiles. "I've decided to go back in time with this fine woman."

Mark is shocked. "You're going back?"

"Why not? I've got alimony due. Maybe I could stay here and get a date with Stax, but this one's a great lay, and she doesn't talk much."

"She's married."

"We'll figure it out. Besides, she says his name is Leofric. I did get that much out of her. The jerk sounds like a bigger pansy than Trotsky."

"He's like the head honcho back there. She hated

his tax increases, so he told her he would lower them if she rode naked."

"Sounds like irreconcilable differences to me."

"She has a ton of kids." Mark holds up nine digits.

"Whoa! fantastic body for that much action! Those brats can bunk with Leofric. We'll work on number ten."

"She's very pious."

"I love pie."

Miss February studies the contents of the shopping cart. "Steve, you figure on becoming a doctor back there?"

"She's smart, Mark. You should keep her. My mother always wanted me to be a doctor. My father just wanted me to stay out of jail. I disappointed both. These will be miracle drugs in whatever year she's from. And I spent a semester in pre-med at Western Kentucky before I flunked out."

"I think you once told me you really majored in partying."

"Yeah. Wish I could remember it."

February calls up the Coventry Street. Godiva smiles. "Home."

Mark helps Steve lift the shopping cart up on the stage. "Steve, it's smart to take the Twinkies. I don't think they're available yet in the 11th century."

"The best thing is that I left a note at the CVS and told them to charge this stuff to my ex-wives."

As Lady G and her steed are positioned, Biff LaFolluvette, and Nan Carpy slither into the room with Biff favoring his sore ass. SWAT had finally breached the front entrance about 30 minutes earlier. They made contact with the rear guard and sent medical help to the wounded. Then, when they turned their attention to Hotwad, because anyone with their head sticking out of a dead T-Rex just seems suspicious, members of the Lewisburg media horde slipped inside as Hotwad was extracted and hauled off for questioning.

"Really Love?" lectures Biff. "A naked broad and a horse."

"Pervert! Pervert! Pervert!" shrieks Nan Carpy like a deranged parrot.

Steve looks toward Biff. "Biffy! Scared of naked women? You should be." Steve whispers toward his new love then points to Biff. Lady Godiva slides off her horse, jumps down on the floor, kisses Steve on the cheek and zeroes in on the news director of Lewisburg's number four station who, if he were smart, would have a camera person with him at this moment.

"Stay away, you naked bitch," yells a concerned Biff. The lady continues and unleashes a vicious kick with her right foot into Biff's crotch causing him to crumble into a blubbery heap.

I wonder where she got those ankle boots,

thinks February.

"Leave him alone you whore," yells Carpy, shoving Lady G on the breasts then pausing for a moment to think she might like the feeling. Godiva counters with a perfect roundhouse right into the harpy's mouth, dropping Carpy unconscious on top of Biff, spitting out blood and yellow teeth during her fall.

"What a woman!" shouts Steve.

Now, it is time for two old friends to part. They shake hands, as they don't believe men should hug. "Marcus. Do you think we'll meet again?"

"Somehow, I think so." They salute each other. "Good job today, Private Love. We finally had some fun at work."

"That much is certain, Private Right. Remember, when your script gets produced, don't let Seth Rogan play me. Good Lord, what he did to the *Green Hornet* was a crime. And tell Dick to kiss my ass." Steve jumps up on the stage, and ten seconds later he belongs to the ages. Mark sadly walks over to the counter and looks at February, "I've lost a friend."

"And gained one."

He writes a couple of dates on a piece of paper. Company is coming, and we've got a couple more things to do before the CIA shows up to claim this place. Do the top one first." February enters data, and Beth Marie Shoreham appears on stage about to climb into a Range Rover. She wears a fetching

TIME MALL

summer dress in a floral print. Mark picks up Stalin's admirals' hat, places it on his head and saunters over. "Beth Marie."

"Mark? Mark Right?"

Mark points to his head. "I finally made admiral. Just like you requested."

She laughs. "What's going on?"

"Listen carefully. Your brakes are out. Do not drive that Range Rover."

"It's brand new."

"Garmon has sabotaged it. He has a big insurance policy on you and needs cash. If you don't believe me, call Butch from the garage to come out and check it. Promise me you won't drive it."

"I promise."

He tips his cap. "I'll talk to you later." Mark sails the hat across the room and nods toward February. Beth Marie disappears and is replaced by the image of a mobile home with an attached deck. A small, meowing kitten, white with black splotches like a Holstein, struggles to climb the steps. Mark hastens into the image, picks up the kitten and kisses it on the head. "Hi, Moo. Let's do another eighteen." As the ten seconds count away, a younger version of Mark points his head out of the door trying to find the source of the meowing.

A happy Mark sets the kitten on the counter. "She's cute," says Miss February. "The kitten. I don't know about Beth Marie."

"We'll figure it out."

Garmon Spooneybarger limps into the room. "Right! You've ruined my mall!"

"Hey, Spooney. You just missed your pal, Joey."

"I decided to end my association with that person."

"After I shot you in the ass. Good thing you had your red pants on. Probably red panties too."

"I see you finally got a little pussy. How long did it take? Thirty years?"

"If only you had not brought the French cut green beans here to spite me, I would have probably been eaten by a dinosaur."

"I know you ratted me out." A cell ring sounds out from Garmon's pocket. "That's my private phone. Nobody has that number. Hello? What? What? I, I, I what?" He ends the call with a shocked look on his face.

"Who was that?" laughs Mark.

"Beth Marie. She's not dead. In fact, she says she's divorcing me and taking this mall."

Mark wonders how the mall could still exist if Beth Marie is back but decides the matter is too complex to worry about at the moment.

Garmon continues. "I'm broke. Mark, old buddy, you've got to get Stalin back here. I have a signed contract."

"Spooney, you're too frazzled. You need to

take a nap."

"I don't have time for a damned nap!"

"Yes, you do." Mark smashes him in the face with a right and pushes him on top of Biff and Nan. "Man, the trash is really piling up around here."

Burley Dick arrives and spots the fallen trio. "You killing people now, Right? It doesn't surprise me."

"I've killed some people today, but not those three."

"W.I.L.—where is Love? I saw what he did in my car."

"He's in 11th century Coventry with Lady Godiva."

"That guy would go anywhere to see a naked woman."

"And he told you to K.M.A!" Mark is relishing the moment.

"What does that mean?"

"Kiss my ass!"

"You two are fir…"

"No, we're not. We quit, Dick!"

February thinks to herself, *I hope I never quit dick.*

Mark steps behind the counter and whispers into February's ear. "Hey, Dick! Say hello to my little friend." The pair let go with a shrill whistle summoning the Albertodormeus into the room via the hole in the wall and watching as he unleashes his mighty stream saturating Burley Dick.

Mark and February laugh. Moo hisses at the dinosaur. Miss February points at Burley Dick. "There

Mark, is that a man soaked in dinosaur piss?"

"Yeah, you damn right that's a man soaked in dinosaur piss."

Mark and February embrace, but there is still a question to be asked. "Miss February, what is your real name?"

"Lisa Gherardini."

"Hello, Lisa. You doing anything tonight?" They kiss as several figures wearing black trench coats appear in the doorway.

"Talk about your basic black," says Lisa.

"Time to sign a nondisclosure agreement, pick up Larry's knife and Steve's picture with Lady Godiva, take Moo home and then ignore the NDA and write a screenplay," smiles Mark.

CHAPTER 17
Two Years Later

It's movie premiere day at the multi-plex in Beth Marie's Mega Mall, formerly the Taj Ma-Mall. The new film is called *Time Mall: The True Story*. The screenplay is written by Mark Right, who was granted an exclusive to the story by Beth Marie Shoreham. The south wing of the mall now ends just past the cinema, the rest of the wing having been walled off by the CIA with Catgrass Creek flowing in through a thick steel grate.

The events of that long day at the mall are somewhat controversial. Many claim that the fantastic stories are a hoax. Of course, this is a lot of the same crowd that believes the 2022 elections in Arizona were legitimate. Evidence has been suppressed, although the Wolf Network did air a special called *Sergei Autopsy*. It was mocked and ridiculed as being a fake. All mall security tapes were confiscated by the CIA, and the bodies of the T-Rexes were quickly hauled away by elements of the deep state. But leftists have still gathered outside the mall protesting the killing of the dinosaurs. The Albertodormeus can be seen in comfortable surroundings in his home at the Lewisburg Zoo where he is billed as a new species discovered in New Guinea, and visitors are advised to keep 30 feet away. Dinosaur brats visiting the zoo predictably named him "Albert."

Ironically, New Guinea is where Hotwad was sent by his rich father on a kayaking vacation, with a custom-built elongated kayak, so he could decompress from the trauma of Stalin falling on his head and being trapped inside a dead dinosaur. He has not been seen since. It is believed he ran into cannibals á la Michael Rockefeller from back in the day. But, to the discriminating cannibal palate, Oysters Rockefeller was likely much more delectable than Oysters Hotwad.

One event of that raucous day cannot be denied. It seems the cell phone salesman punched by Stalin remained in the mall throughout and recorded the fight between Miss February and Miss October on his phone. Once posted to the internet, it became a viral sensation, and Lisa Gherardini received many offers to appear in professional wrestling, which she is considering. She is also the new spokesperson for Jones Bootmaker and is helping them develop a line of thick-soled ankle boots called Godiva's Gonad Gnashers.

TIME MALL

There is much anticipation for this movie. National media is present as well as the top three stations in Lewisburg. WDOA has been banned from the event. In the past two years, Channel 82 has fallen into the number five position, ranking behind an all-graphics channel of scrolling public events. Biff LaFolluvette and Nan Carpy are still mismanaging the news department. But Burley Dick has been fired, as Phil Veal did not like the sight of him drenched in dinosaur piss. Dick is now the assistant manager of the number six carwash in Lewisburg and is required to wear khaki pants and a blue oxford shirt on the job.

The theatre lobby is packed for the event. The eleven available calendar girls are there and participating. Kohl's, anticipating that the movie will be a hit (It will be), has signed nine of them to a contract and outfitted them in a new line of evening wear. The non-Kohl's participants are Lisa Gherardini, who has enough of her own deals, and Lorna Juner, who wanted something better than Kohl's.

Men in tuxedos and women in elegant gowns abound. Costumed characters are all about. Stalin's admiral's cap and corncob pipe are on display. A unique champagne fountain, in the shape of the Albertodormeus, dispenses the bubbly from a delicate area of its anatomy. With the approval of Mark and Beth Marie, several people have product tables and are autographing their own creations. One is

Larry Biggs, who has topped off his short-sleeved oxford shirt with a formal bow tie, signing copies of his new book *I Hate That Bitch: My 40 plus years of watching The Andy Griffith Show*. He has already made enough money from the tome to quit his full-time job at WDOA but still works there one day a week to keep Aunt Bea off the air as much as possible.

Larry also has a new business in the mall. It turns out that Bolsheviky did not need a new manager, as Beth Marie shut it down and sold the contents at a premium price to the Lewisburg Democratic party. With plenty of money and his old home space available, Larry snatched up the spot to open a bar and grille called Godiva's Dive. The joint features a life-sized blow up of Steve Love's pose with Lady Godiva, copies of famous, classy paintings of the naked lady, including John Collier's 1895 masterpiece, and pictures of characters from *The Andy Griffith Show* (except for one.) Larry's bowie knife is also on display. Monday evening is especially busy there as that is 10 cent wing night.

Beside Larry in a comfortable cage is Moo the cat, all grown up for the second time. Her fame is about to take off, and as people see the movie, she will become known as Moo the Time Cat and be offered many cat food commercials and her own film called "Time Mall: The Kitty Story." Larry is feeding her Whiskas Temptations and delightful salmon croquets from the buffet table. That spread was put together by Grace Chan (January) and Lumina Salazar (November) as this is the first event for their new catering company Graceful Luminance.

Stax Spankster (August) is signing DVD covers of her unauthorized movie *Time Mall: The Titty Story*, and it's six sequels. No longer interested in being on *60 Minutes*, she intends to make 60 sequels. She was too busy to appear in the official *Time Mall* movie, so her little sister Panty-free Spankster was cast.

Jessica Striker is running a recruiting kiosk for the Army. Even though the media has denied that the battle of the Taj Ma-Mall happened, the Army believed the tales of Jessica's valor that leaked out and gave her a commission as a Captain then made her a full-time recruiting officer stationed at the mall. For this event, she was allowed to wear an army green Kohl's gown along with her red, white and blue helmet and boots.

Aria Stanzer (May) is signing autographs. She has become very popular after winning the Lewisburg Derby on a horse named T-Rex. Verbota Tubbs (September) and Lorna Juner (June) have a table to sell their joint calendar but are spending a lot of time at the champagne fountain.

After getting a look at how slim her butt was with a chunk missing, Hilda Gast (December) went on a diet and lost 40 pounds, so she is signing her controversial diet book, *The Slice Your Butt Off Diet*. The flowers for the event were brought in by Yvonne Lunde (April) and displays of books about historical people sighted at the mall were set up by Emma Fleet (March), who has continued to wear her hair down.

There is one more person on hand to sign copies of a new book. When the bodies of the Sergeis were gathered, one was found to be alive. This was the one Lisa Gheradini had disarmed. After recovering, he received prosthetics at taxpayers' expense, improved his English and decided to defect to the West, adopting the name Sergei Freedom. His book, *I'd Rather Not Be Red When I Come Back from The Dead*, chronicles his life growing up in Georgia with an entrepreneurial spirit. His first business venture was renting his pet sheep, Ivan the Fluffable, out on dates. Then he made good coin selling half smoked cigarettes, usually gleaned from the floor of the local meeting hall after the Tsarist police busted up a gathering of social revolutionaries. Later, he cleaned up peddling used babushka undergarments to local creeps. During this venture, he bought low and sold high. In the book, he also rallies against his abuse at the hands of Stalin, praises the business opportunities he has found in the 21st century and pledges to pay back the costs of his new arms and hands. Currently, he is the manager of that number six carwash in Lewisburg and loves to harangue Burley Dick in obscure Georgian dialects.

A buzz arises as Mark Right enters the lobby wearing a classic black tuxedo from Brooks Brothers, a Jos. A. Bank shirt with a Calvin Klein tie, and Johnston and Murphy dress shoes. On his left arm is Beth Marie Shoreham, looking stunning in a powder blue, shimmering, sleeveless gown overnighted from Bloomingdale's. The right arm is enhanced with Lisa Gheradini, knocking them dead with a beaded camo sleeveless gown that was custom made. She is shod, of course, in her brown boots from Jones Bootmaker. They have all three been so busy the past two years that they are just good friends at this point. "Hey, Mark!" shouts Larry. "Nice pair!"

"Hey, Larry! Hey, Moo!"

"Thanks again for getting my knife back, Mark."

"Thanks again for putting it there. It came in handy."

After a round of pictures, Beth Marie breaks off to confer with Grace and Lumina about the buffet. Mark and Lisa step in front of a bank of microphones, and the newly minted screenwriter addresses the throng. "Hello everyone. Thanks for coming out today. We actually have two great movies showing. *Time Mall* is on 19 screens and on the other screen we have arranged for a special re-release of one of my favorites. It's Guy Ritchie's incredible 2015 film, *The Man from U.N.C.L.E.* An underappreciated masterpiece that deserves a shot at a wider audience. Now.

Questions?"

"Mr. Right, are you happy with how *Time Mall* the movie came out?"

"For the most part. We did have problems with one actor wanting to ad-lib when he didn't need to because he had such a great script to work from."

"Right, what made you think that you had any business being a screenwriter. That job takes talent, which you don't have."

"Meow, did a WDOA reporter sneak in here? Listen it's screenwriting-duh! It's not like curing cancer."

"Lisa, are we going to see you in the wresting ring soon?"

"You just might. I'm trying to come up with the perfect costume to go with my ass-kicking boots from Jones Bootmaker."

"Mark, it is rumored that when you were on the movie set you got very friendly with the twelve young actresses playing the calendar girls."

Mark feels Lisa staring at him. "I can assure you that everything was very professional. Yes, that is it."

"Mark, is it true you're being played by Stephen Baldwin in the movie?"

"Yes, the character based on me is portrayed by the handsome and talented Mr. Baldwin. He is the best Baldwin brother, and the only one we really need in our society."

"Mr. Right, the uber-creative videographer J.P.

Forte is missing. You say he went back in time with Stalin. I think you might have murdered him because you were jealous of all his awards."

"Wow. Quite an accusation from the oldest reporter in the room. Forte's awards, really? Golden Links and Bronze Knobs, who cares? And I'm convinced he bought his regional Emmy off eBay. Or—let's see, you have like a thousand regional Emmys, maybe you sold him one."

"Come on, it's only 127, and I would never sell one."

"You probably can't give them away. But I'm not jealous of you. I like to make fun of you because you're so sanctimonious, but I'm not jealous. Look at Stax Spankster, and let's do, she has won seven best actress 'Boobster' awards for her *Time Mall* movies. A great series by the way. I'm not jealous of her. No, I would not have killed J.P. Forte because I want him to be alive. I want him to be alive and humiliated by having to fetch oak leaves for Stalin."

"What are you talking about?"

"You'll know after you see the movie."

"Mark, who is playing your friend Steve Love in the movie?"

"You people don't follow the trades at all do you? I don't think Steve would be happy with the actor cast in that role. I tried to talk the producers out of it, but they insisted."

Theatre #7

Time Mall's first showing of the day is playing before a packed house. On the screen Stephen Baldwin as Mark and Seth Rogan as Steve are lying on a pile of padded bras and thongs.

"Oh, God … What happened? I feel like Melissa McCarthy is sitting on my head."

"Wow, bro! That was intense."

"While we're flying through the air, I thought we were going to wake up as roommates in hell."

"Dude! I need to spark one up."

In the audience is Christopher Columbus eating from a large tub of popcorn. He is working as a waiter in a new Columbus themed restaurant in the mall called Cristobal's. Patrons often ask him to pose for pictures because of his resemblance to the painting of Columbus on the wall. He lives in the employee apartments constructed in the east wing by Beth Marie, instead of a silly amusement park. On off days, he attends movies or sails toy boats on Catgrass Creek. He is enjoying the movie and has only one comment, "This is the shit, dude."

Of course, one is left to wonder.

1492
On Board the Santa Maria

The new world is approaching on the horizon, but the crew of the Santa Maria has gathered mid-ship to stare at their captain who does not seem to be himself or even look like himself.

"Hi guys. I don't think I'm supposed to be here. Does anyone have a cell phone I can use? Can't get a signal on mine. I need to call my agent. Oh, can you cash an Old Navy paycheck on this ship? At least I started working there on pay day. Am I right? Guys? Guys? Whoa! This is the shit, dude."

Back at the Press Conference

"Mark, in the movie are we going to see Davy Crockett fly out of the alamo on a jetpack?"

"We are. And Nick Searcy did a fantastic job playing Davy Crockett by the way."

"That's just ridiculous."

"Well, the history books seem to have some changes now. There are Crockett sightings for years after 1836. And there's the story that after the Alamo, Davy Crockett rejoined Sam Houston's army under an assumed name and fought in the Battle of San Jacinto helping to crush Santa Ana." Mark pounds his right fist into his left hand.

"Why would he take an assumed name?"

"Maybe just simple modesty."

"If Davy took a jetpack back to the alamo, what happened to it."

"It would be interesting to find out."

"Mark, I will admit that there are some changes in the history books. They now say that General Patton walked away from his car accident but then went into a quiet retirement. Does that seem right?"

"Not really. I can't imagine him being quiet. There must be more to it."

"After what you claim happened here there doesn't seem to be any change in the history of the Soviet Union."

"Maybe it hasn't happened yet. This time stuff is tricky."

On the other side of the lobby, the one-time Abraham Lincoln actor approaches a group of young women. This time he is dressed as Stalin with the grey uniform and Admiral's cap. "Hi, girls, I'm afraid I'm going to have to arrest you and drag you off to see my private gulag."

From the other direction approaches the former George Washington Carver actor, also dressed as Stalin. "Forget him, ladies. I'm black Stalin, and my gulag is much bigger than his."

"Get lost! Stalin can't be black."

"He can be, and he is. He is also sexy as hell."

"I'm going to purge your black ass."

The two swing and miss at each other and are soon wresting around on the floor. Beth Marie spots the melee and calls for security. Chuck and Bob, now wanting to be called Charles and Robert, flash onto the scene sporting charcoal-grey dockers and yellow turtlenecks from Land's End along with mauve blazers via Botany 500, finished off with black Doc Martens. They have weapons under their jackets and no eye patches, as Beth Marie paid for surgery to repair the sight in their damaged eyes. The two bad actors are quickly collared and hauled off, to the applause of the crowd.

The press conference resumes. "Lisa, did you see Lady Godiva here at the mall?"

"I did."

"What did you think about her?"

"She was a beautiful woman who was very confident in her nudity."

"You were pretty confidant being topless in that viral video."

"That much is certain," she grins as Mark smiles at her.

"So, Mark, you claim Steve Love went back with Lady Godiva, but most of us think he is in hiding to avoid alimony payments."

"He's back there. Trust me. He took a bunch of stuff from CVS with him, so he could become a doctor."

"About that doctor thing. Some history books now mention a physician being burned at the stake in Coventry in the early 11th century. Care to comment?"

"It couldn't be Steve. He's too smart for that. I'm sure he's fine."

Coventry, England
The Early 11th Century

Steve Love enters his home after a long day at work, he wears an 11th century physician's gown and brown leather boots manufactured by a local cobbler whom he is treating for several putrid illnesses. He and Lady Godiva, after her messy divorce, have settled down in a cute stone cottage, which was one of Godiva's many property holdings, far from any graveyards or pestilence pits, not that those things are needed with Steve as the town doctor. He tosses his cap and medical bag on the dining table as he sits down on a crude but sturdy wooden chair. "Hey baby, I'm home."

Lady Godiva emerges from the back, naked and carrying a roast goose on a platter. She clomps over to him, her ankle boots striking against the uneven stone floor. Steve has been trying to teach her modern English, and she is now speaking in a kind of mock Cockney accent. Maybe this is where the cockney accent came from. And she is speaking a lot. "Ah …

me love. It's good to see ya."

"Put down that goose, and I'll give you a goose."

"Ah, ya fla'er me you do."

She sets down the goose and jumps on his lap eliciting a groan. "I think I know where all those Twinkies went."

"Me old 'usband was 'ere today."

"Is he still trying to get you to put on a dress?"

"E be claimin' you be in league with the devil. Sayin' they going to be a burnin' ya at the stake 'e is."

"That ungrateful bastard. I'm the best doctor this town has ever had."

"That ya be."

"No one's even died since I came here. Well, except for old MacGregor."

"Ah, stupid ol' MacGrega. That big idget. E be all drunk and singin' and wandering in the street a crapin' his pantaloons. Then 'e gets hit by me ex-husband's carriage! That was rich it was."

"If I could have gotten there sooner."

"E was spread all about, love. Nothin but pieces left. They fed 'im to the 'ogs they did." There is a knock at the door. "That be ol' Leofric now."

"I'll prescribe Leo a laxative. That should clear this up. Then we'll eat that goose and take another shot at number 10."

"I can 'ardley wait."

Steve gets up to answer the door.

Back in the 21st Century

The press conference is over, and Lisa and Mark are checking out the sights in the lobby. They are approached by Verbota Tubbs and Lorna Juner, each drinking a glass of champagne. Kohl's has dressed Verbota in a short-sleeved orange gown that she has accessorized with her own pair of vintage Air Jordan's. Lorna has scammed a silvery, strapless, Oscar de La Renta number which clashes with her standard green heels.

"Hi, Mark guy and Miss Feberoary," slurs Lorna. "Remember ush."

"Of course," Mark answers. "You two never got along very well."

"We're best friends now," says Verbota.

"Buddies, even," slobbers Lorna as the two put their left arms around each other.

"You ladies look lovely tonight," compliments Lisa.

"My gown cost two thousand hundred dollars," proclaims Lorna. "I'm taking it back tomorrow, so I don't have to pay for it."

"We have our own calendar now," Verbota tells them.

"I saw it," says Mark. "Looks good."

Lorna Juner is teetering on her heels. "It's called Ebola and Ebonics!"

"It's 'Ebony and Ivory', you stupid bitch."

"Don't bitch me, bitch." Lorna tosses her drink in Verbota's face, and Ms. Tubbs returns the favor.

"You got champagne on my gown! Now I can't return it!" They slap each other and are soon rolling around on the floor pulling hair and tugging at bodices. Lisa puts a hand over Mark's eyes. Beth Marie calls for security. Charles and Robert jet out to do their thing, having to tuck a couple of exposed boobs back in as they hustle the two pairs away.

Then Beth Marie issues another order to get the champagne cleaned up. "Spooneybarger! Cleanup!" Garmon Spooneybarger quickly emerges from the back wearing a janitor's uniform and carrying a mop.

"Looking good, Spooney," shouts Mark.

"Shut up, Right. You look like a retarded penguin."

"And you look like you've found your calling."

"Beth Marie," pleads Garmon. "I need a raise."

"Beth Marie glowers at him. "Shut up, mop up, get lost."

Garmon swings the mop and mutters to himself. "I hope Nelson doesn't see me like this."

A few minutes later, Beth Marie shouts to Mark and Lisa. "Over here! The feed is about to come in from the Louvre."

In honor of Leonardo DaVinci, a video feed of the Mona Lisa has been arranged. The smiling one is fresh off a new restoration, and her colors are said to be more vivid than ever.

History's favorite lady now appears on the large video screen. Mark, Lisa and Beth Marie are stunned. After a long pause Mark looks at Lisa. "When I first saw you, I thought you looked familiar, but I never realized you looked so much like the Mona Lisa."

"Neither did I."

"I think I know now what Leonardo had in that sketch pad. Too bad he didn't go with the camo bikini," rues Mark.

"For sure, I would never wear that gown."

"What's that just barely sticking out of her hand," asks Beth Marie. "It's round and looks like brass."

"Looks like the cap of a shotgun shell," observes Mark.

"Yeah," states Lisa. "Federal. 12-gauge, #4 buckshot."

Searching for something, Mark can only think of one thing. "Like our friend Alvin C. York said, 'the Lord sure do work in mysterious ways.'"

"And so do Mr. Da Vinci," smiles the face of the Mona Lisa."

Epilogue

1923
The Countryside near Gori, Georgia

Stalin and company have been back in the USSR for about two hours. The mighty ass has taken Channing Gingham (October) to the cabin where he lectured the Sergeis. There is a moderate blaze in the fireplace they are standing in front of, but Channing is shivering, still clad in her ice cream-stained red bikini and standing on the scuffed Christian Louboutin's. She has found a ratty pelt on the floor and is trying to draw it around her shoulders, the dust from the mangy fur grinding into her cuts and abrasions. There is still dried blood, Neapolitan ice cream, and chocolate syrup on her face. Stalin has his left hand wrapped in a bloody, filthy rag and his uniform stained red at the left shoulder.

Channing is not happy. "What is this place? Why is it so cold? You said it was spring. Is there a woman's clothing store around here? Where the hell is

Trotsky? He said I could wear his helmet to keep my ears warm.

"He look like idiot in dumb, metal bonnet."

"Why don't you move your mighty ass and find me something to eat?"

"Stop mooing, you stupid American cow. I lose hat. That more important."

"More important than your finger?"

"I have more fingers. I no have hat." He reaches his right hand into a pocket and retrieves the driver's licenses of Mark and Steve. "These two cause all the badness. Mark Right and Steve Love. I will get more Sergeis. I will train them to fight instead of speak English gooder. Yes, that is it. I will be more cleverer. Then somehow. Somewhere in time. I find Mark Right and Steve Love, and I kill them." He returns the licenses to his pocket with a scowl on his face.

"Don't forget that February bitch that attacked me for no reason. I want to kill her."

"You will get to kill her after I make her plow Ukraine."

J.P. Forte enters, walking gingerly, with his camera on his shoulder. He takes the tarnished bronze knob award out of his camera bag and sets it on the fireplace mantel. "That should class this dump up. By the way, mighty ass, I need to charge my batteries. Do you even have electricity in this cocked-up fuckpile of a country?"

Stalin scratches his behind. "Damnable, itchable ass." Then he heads toward the door starting to unfasten his pants. "Oak Leaves, Forte. Bring me oak leaves."

Forte shakes his head. "Oy-fucking-vai!"